ALL THINGS HIDDEN

HOME TO HEATHER CREEK

ALL THINGS HIDDEN

Tricia Goyer

Home to Heather Creek is a trademark of Guideposts.

Copyright © 2023 by Guideposts. All rights reserved.

This book, or parts thereof, may not be reproduced, stored in a retrieval system, or transmitted in any form or by any means, electronic, mechanical, photocopying, recording, or otherwise, without the written permission of the publisher.

The characters and events in this book are fictional, and any resemblance to actual persons or events is coincidental.

Scripture quotations in this volume are taken from the *The Holy Bible, New International Version* (NIV). Copyright © 1973, 1978, 1984, 2011 by Biblica, Inc. Used by permission of Zondervan. All rights reserved worldwide.

Published by Guideposts
100 Reserve Road, Suite E200
Danbury, CT 06810
Guideposts.org

Cover by Lookout Design, Inc.
Interior design by Cindy LaBreacht
Additional design work by Müllerhaus
Typeset by Aptara, Inc.

ISBN 978-1-961125-10-0 (hardcover)
ISBN 978-1-961125-12-4 (epub)

Printed in the United States of America
10 9 8 7 6 5 4 3 2 1

To Andrea, my Czech daughter
God gave us that gift of you!
and
To Stacey, my sweet sister
Digging in family history pays off. I now have you!

Acknowledgments

I'm very thankful that God has given me such an amazing group of people to share my life with. My words and work wouldn't be the same without their input into my life!

John, thank you for the big things (like loving me unconditionally) and the small things (like loading the dishwasher and putting away laundry). You are a gift to me. I love sharing life (and sometimes chores) with you! Cory, Leslie, Nathan and Andrea . . . you rock. I love that God gave us an extra kid from halfway around the world. How cool is that? Grandma, thank you for sharing our family's story in many ways. Thank you for your love. Amy Lathrop, thank you for walking through the publishing journey with me. You're a dear friend and an awesome assistant. Loring Morris, see . . . I told you I think about you all the time. Thank you for living your life in Uganda and being an example to me of faithful service. Easthaven Baptist Church, especially our small group: Job and Marie Dittmer, Steve and Karlene Waltman, Greg and Jan Griffin, Pat and Shelly Callan, and Joe Evich. You are the best church friends ever! My agent, Janet Kobobel Grant, thank you for listening every time I say, "Janet, I have an idea." Keith Edwards, thank you for sharing your stories about your parents as settlers, and for the research book "A Gathering of Memories" that brought history to life for me! Beth Adams and Fiona Serpa, thank you for showing me how to make a good story great . . . and helping me get there! Finally, thank you to my Twitter friends who voted on the title. Glad you liked it!

—Tricia Goyer

Home to Heather Creek

Before the Dawn

Sweet September

Circle of Grace

Homespun Harvest

A Patchwork Christmas

An Abundance of Blessings

Every Sunrise

The Promise of Spring

April's Hope

Seeds of Faith

On the Right Path

Sunflower Serenade

Second Chances

Prayers and Promises

Giving Thanks

Holiday Homecoming

Family Matters

All Things Hidden

ALL THINGS HIDDEN

Chapter One

Large icicles dripped from the overhang of Bedford Community Church just as they had for more then one hundred years. Charlotte tucked the green bean casserole closer to her as she ducked, trying to miss the drips of water. It didn't work, and an icy drop hit the back of her neck and dribbled down her back.

"Oh, bother." She wiped the back of her neck and hurried to the fellowship hall for a special meeting of the Women's Group. Charlotte glanced at her watch and sighed. She was thirty minutes late, which meant she most likely had missed out on Melody Givens's potato salad, made from her great-grandmother's recipe. It always went first.

She moved to the long folding table, which was covered with a faded plastic tablecloth. Bowls and platters of various sizes covered its surface. Most of them were half-empty, all except Melody's large, blue potato salad bowl, which was scraped clean. Seeing the bowl nearly caused tears to well up in Charlotte's eyes—but not because she had missed the salad. It was more that she was thankful Melody was on the mend. Melody's recent fight against breast cancer had reminded Charlotte how quickly life can change, seemingly overnight.

Charlotte placed her casserole on the table and scanned the room, looking for an empty space to sit. Nearly all the folding chairs were filled with brightly bundled churchwomen. Perhaps the hint of warm air and the sunshine casting long arms over the vast prairie had drawn everyone from their winter hibernation. Either that or the curious postcard Hannah had sent out to all the church ladies, hinting of a fun surprise to be revealed at today's luncheon. That had been enough to stir Charlotte from her home even though she hadn't finished up Sam's birthday preparations.

The noise of ladies' voices rose and bounced around the room like lottery balls in a glass box. Charlotte's stomach rumbled, adding to the noise, and she scanned the food. She'd attended enough church potlucks—or smorgasbords, as Pastor Evans called them—to know which serving dish belonged to whom. And equally telltale was the offering inside. Celia Potts's potato-sausage casserole. Andrea Vink's pigs in a blanket. Anita Wilson's almond coffee bread.

Charlotte took a serving of each. Then her lips puckered into a reined-in smile as she remembered Bob's comment at the last church potluck: "I have no doubt that God's heavenly feast won't start until Mary Louise Henner sets her plate of Swedish meatballs in cream-of-mushroom soup on God's banquet table."

Charlotte spotted an empty chair in the back of the room. She quickly finished filling her plate and then hurried in that direction. Before she got there, a hand gently grabbed her wrist. Charlotte paused. She glanced down, spotting Melody.

"I couldn't save you a seat, but I saved you this." She lifted a small paper plate with a scoop of potato salad. "I had to protect it with my life."

"Thank you! I owe you one." Charlotte took the plate with her free hand and settled into a chair at a table filled with some of the older ladies. She'd just taken her first bite of potato salad when the pastor's wife, Nancy Evans, rose.

"Okay, ladies." Nancy flapped her hands in the air, reminding Charlotte of hummingbird wings. The voices stilled in record time, and all eyes turned to the front.

"Now, I know we usually share upcoming events at the end of the meeting, but I also know you're all eager to hear about our surprise project. So, Hannah, would you please head up here and share just what the ladies of Bedford Community Church are going to be up to?"

Hannah hurried to the front of the room. In her hand she held an old book. Charlotte leaned forward, trying to get a better look. The burgundy cover looked familiar. She bit her lower lip as she remembered where she'd seen it before. It was one of the old hymnals the church had used when her kids were small. Just spotting the cover with the embossed cross and gold lettering took her mind back to the days when her three kids lined up in the pew, their short legs sticking straight out. Charlotte would pass out sheets of lined paper and colored pencils in an attempt to keep Bill, Denise, and Pete occupied during the long sermon. *How many pictures of cows and sheep, horses and tractors had been drawn, using those old hymnals as lap tables?*

Her bottom lip pouted at days gone past as she remembered Bill and Denise playing hangman and tic-tac-toe. Then there was Pete, who'd been more interested in writing in the book. He always did find a way to get into trouble —even sitting in a church pew.

"Hello, ladies."

Charlotte snapped back to the present at the sound of her best friend's voice.

"It's great to have so many of you here." Hannah Carter's whole face lit up as she stood in the center of the fellowship hall, looking like a four-year-old at Christmas. "I'm going to start by sharing something I found in our own church basement." Hannah's laughter erupted from her lips. "And you thought it was just the place to stash outdated choir robes. Well, listen to this." She cleared her throat.

> *Now let us climb Nebraska's loftiest mount,*
> *And from its summit view the scenes below.*
> *The moon comes like an angel down from heaven;*
> *Its radiant face is the unclouded sun;*
> *Its outspread wings the over-arching sky;*
> *Its voice the charming minstrels of the air;*
> *Its breath the fragrance of the bright wild-flowers.*
> *Behold the prairie, broad and grand and free—*
> *'Tis God's own garden, unprofaned by man.*

Charlotte paused, the fork halfway to her mouth. A poem? Hannah always came up with creative ways to announce upcoming events, but she'd never done it with a poem before. Charlotte looked around the silent room; it was clear that Hannah had gotten everyone's attention.

"It's a lovely poem," Eulalia Barry commented.

"Can you read it again?" Nancy said from where she stood at the punch bowl. Hannah must not have heard her because she put the poem back inside the Bible and placed it on the table.

"Only problem I saw . . ."—Melody pointed her fork in the air—". . . was where it talked about climbing Nebraska's loftiest mount—unless they mean the haystack over at the Stevenson farm!"

"Sugarloaf Hill *is* a mountain." Eighty-seven-year-old Anita Wilson leaned closer to Charlotte, as if it were her job to defend the highest peak in Adams County.

Nancy Evans tapped her fork against her water glass. "Ladies, attention please. It was a lovely poem, but Hannah does have a purpose for reading it. She's announcing service events, remember?"

The murmurs in the room stilled to a hush. Hannah cleared her throat and continued.

"If you're wondering where I got this poem, it came from a box in the basement—from one of many boxes. The poem is titled 'Nebraska,' and it was written in 1854 by a fellow named George Washington Bungay. The boxes are filled with wonderful things, ladies. I found an old church cookbook, written by the women in our congregation in the 1920s. Can you believe that? There are Sunday-school registers from when my husband, Frank, was just a boy. And Charlotte," Hannah found her among the other faces and focused her gaze. "I found a photo of Bill when he was baptized. What a sweet little thing. Remind me to show you after lunch."

"And the service project is . . ." Nancy's smile spread like butter melting in the sun. She cocked one eyebrow and motioned with a wave of her hand, encouraging Hannah to continue.

"Oh yes. The point of all this is that Pastor Evans has asked if the women of the church would clean out the basement. It was due for a spring cleaning at least a quarter of a century ago." Hannah chuckled at her own joke. "He also asked that we go through the items and create a display for the 130th anniversary of the founding of the church, which is coming up in about a month."

More murmurs erupted, but this time Hannah wasn't distracted. "Believe it or not, our Bedford Community Church is one of the oldest churches in Adams County!"

Charlotte bit her lip. Even though she did like the poem and was eager to see that photo of Bill, the thought of going through those stacks of boxes in the basement didn't excite her. If she were serious about spring cleaning, she'd start in her *own* basement. It had also been due for a spring cleaning a quarter of a century ago.

"Do you have a time and date set when we'll meet?" Mary Louise asked. Like most of the women, Mary Louise was a farmer's wife and seemed eager for a new project—something different to bring interest to the long winter days.

"How about tomorrow?" Hannah clasped her hands together. "I can be here to open the church, and maybe some of you can swing by after dropping your kids off at school. Or grandkids, if that's the case." Hannah turned and met Charlotte's eyes as she said that.

Charlotte nodded, and she knew to Hannah that was as good as a promise. Truth was, it had been a long and challenging winter for her too. It would be nice to get out of the house and spend some time with friends.

For the next few minutes Hannah discussed the display that would highlight their church history as well as her ideas for a community event celebrating the beginnings of the Bedford Community Church. Rosemary offered to donate an antique display case from her store, and other ladies volunteered to create posters and flyers to invite the community to their open house—or rather, open church.

When Hannah was finished, Nancy Evans took the floor and attempted to go through old business and also to talk about an Easter brunch, but it was no use. Everyone was antsy to get down to the basement and start digging into those boxes. If Hannah had already dug up cookbooks and hymnals, what other treasure might they hold?

"Can we start right now?" Mary Louise piped up as she pushed back her chair.

"I don't see why not," Nancy Evans acquiesced as she absorbed the excitement in the room. "I don't think Hannah would be able to stop everyone now, even if she tried."

"Are you going to join us?" Mary Louise asked Charlotte as she walked toward her.

Charlotte glanced at her watch. Tonight was Sam's birthday—his eighteenth birthday. Even though she'd already baked the cake and left it on the counter to cool, she still wanted to straighten up the house a bit and get dinner started. Everyone was coming over, which meant three times the normal amount of cooking. Three times the people and laughter too.

Yet I would like to take a peek.

"Well, I really should head home after we clean up the lunch mess. There's so much I still have to do today." She bit her lip. "But I suppose I could just poke around for a few minutes. I have to admit I'm intrigued."

Thirty minutes later Charlotte found herself sitting in a chilly basement next to Dana's Grandma Maxine, known as Maxie to everyone in Bedford. Together they sorted through a box of random items. Charlotte reached up and pulled a cobweb out of Maxie's salt-and-pepper hair, which was pulled back in a bun. She flicked the piece of web to the ground.

"This isn't the cleanest place," Charlotte commented.

"No, but the spiders seem to like it." Maxie grinned.

Next to them on the floor Charlotte and Maxie had created three piles: display, save, toss. So far the toss pile had more in it than the other piles.

"Who in the world would have saved a file of old grocery receipts from 1974?" Charlotte mumbled scanning one of the receipts. "Then again I wouldn't mind if Hershey bars cost ten cents again." She closed the file and tossed it into the trash pile.

"What are you doing?" Mary Louise hustled over. Her penciled eyebrows arched. Her hair was reddish-orange—a color that clearly came from a bottle. Mary Louise was now nearing sixty and the color most likely hid gray, but it was the same color Mary Louise had been using since Charlotte met her when they were both new brides. "Are you kidding? Why would you throw away those old receipts? They'd be perfect for June's museum."

"June?" Maxie tilted her head. Her eyes twinkled, and Charlotte realized for the first time that Dana had her grandmother's eyes. "I thought we were going to have the display ready by the end of this month—you know, for the church's anniversary?"

Mary Louise shook her finger just a few inches from Maxie's face. "You know very well that June is my niece, and she's working with Edna from the library on the museum."

"Museum?" Charlotte rubbed her itchy nose. Her hands felt dry and scratchy from handling the old paper. "I haven't heard anything about a museum."

"It's not much to start." Mary Louise scooped up the file of receipts. "They're putting it in one of the old storage rooms they cleared out. June just graduated from Wayne State College, and she's fascinated by Nebraska history. Her hope is to get the old schoolhouse west of town moved into that lot just off Lincoln Street and then have it refurbished."

"That old thing?" Maxie swatted the air. "It should have been demolished long ago."

"Then you need to invite her to join us. She would get a kick out of this," Charlotte said, but Mary Louise wasn't listening. Instead she was already hustling to the other side of the room to rescue more "treasures" out of the throwaway piles.

"Listen to this." Maxie held up a yellowed piece of

newsprint. "It's a story from the *Bedford Leader* from 1940, talking about the history of the Bedford community and our church: 'Every Saturday evening Reverend James McCaughey would ring the school bell, reminding the people of the Sabbath. For homestead families this meant preparation of Sunday school lessons for teachers and students alike. It meant Saturday night baths for children and the pressing of Sunday clothes for the morn. The bell carried the news that soon they'd be meeting with their friends and neighbors—for some it was the only time of the week they left the homestead. Sundays were treasured days.'" Maxie looked up. "There's more here, but isn't that beautiful?"

Charlotte nodded, sneezed, and then rubbed dust from her nose. "I never thought about that before. I suppose Sunday gatherings were very important back then."

"Yes, making the church building even more important." Maxie tilted her head and looked into the distance. "I remember what it was like growing up around these parts. There was a lot of space, and not a whole lot of folks. Getting together was a treat. It's strange to think that the old people that I knew growing up were some of the first homesteaders. They enjoyed the landscape unprofaned by man's hand—as Hannah read from that poem."

"That's right." Charlotte placed the newspaper article in the keep pile. "I remember some of those homesteaders too—or rather their kids who grew up in the area. It's strange to think that their ordinary lives would be so interesting to us now." She laughed. "I should tell my grandkids to appreciate everything around my place that's old, because someday those very things might be worthy of being put into a museum!"

Maxie laughed and then took a photo slide out from one of the boxes and held it up toward the window. "Exactly. I bet if the homesteaders were alive today they'd shrug their shoulders, not understanding how fascinated we are by their oxcarts and soddies."

"Charlotte, you're not going to believe this." Hannah hustled over, waving a newspaper in her hand. "You're not going to believe this," she repeated. When she got closer Charlotte could see the paper in her friend's hand was a front page of the *Harding Tribune*.

"Look here." Hannah pointed to the middle of the front page.

"An advertisement for the Kerr Opera House?" Charlotte tucked a strand of hair behind her ear.

"No, under that. Don't you recognize the name?"

Charlotte squinted and looked closer.

"'Elijah Coleman pleads not guilty to theft charges,'" Maxie read out loud. Her eyes widened, and she turned to Charlotte. "Oh my, I remember this story."

Hearing the name, Charlotte felt her stomach tighten, as if the potato salad she'd eaten had turned into one solid rock.

"Charlotte?" Mary Louise hurried back over and took her hand. "Are you all right? The color just washed from your face. Do you need a glass of water?"

Charlotte nodded, but she didn't know how to explain. She turned to Hannah, opened her mouth, and closed it again, seeking help.

"Elijah Coleman is one of Charlotte's relatives," Hannah stated matter-of-factly. "I remember hearing about him once or twice, but I never heard anything like this."

"Yes, Mary Louise, Maxie," Charlotte confessed. "He was my great-grandfather. And he was accused of being a thief." Charlotte sighed. "The community members said he took the very funds that had been set aside to build Bedford Community Church."

Chapter Two

Sam took the dollar bill and pressed it on his leg, attempting to smooth it out. He then tried sliding it into the soda machine slot again. His mouth was dry, and he needed caffeine to stay awake. He'd stayed up too late last night thinking about things—about turning eighteen, about his mom, his past, his future. Too much thinking, not enough sleep. "Come on, come on, you stupid thing."

The machine sucked in the dollar, whirred for a minute, and then slid it back out. "This stinks." He glanced at his watch, wondering if he had enough time to run to the office, beg for change, and then run back.

Unfortunately he only had a minute before the bell, and he doubted his teachers would fall for the it's-my-birthday-give-me-a-break plea. It seemed that he was the only one who thought turning eighteen—becoming an adult—was a big deal. His grandparents hadn't even said much about it. His siblings hadn't either. And he doubted his dad even remembered what day he had been born. "One more time, machine. It's my birthday. Treat me nice," Sam mumbled out loud.

"Need change?" Sam felt a soft hand on his arm. He turned and noticed a girl standing beside him. He recognized her from around school and thought her name was Kendall.

"Yeah, do you have any? That would be sweet."

"Sure." The girl snapped open a coin purse, dumped some change into her hand, and then held it out for him to pick through. He took four quarters and then placed his dollar in her hand.

"My mom used to have a coin purse like that." *She used to dump her money in her hand like that too.*

"Did she get rid of it?" Kendall smiled.

He turned back to the soda machine, sliding in the coins, listening to their jingle and clunk as they made their way through the mechanism until finally clinking to a stop. He pushed the button for Dr. Pepper.

"Actually, she died a couple years ago," he said, barely loud enough to be heard over the sound of the soda can tumbling into the tray.

"That's sad. I'm sorry, Sam. I know how it feels. My mom died too. When I was eight."

Sam grabbed his soda and turned to her, his eyes widening in interest. He didn't know what was most surprising—her stating so plainly that her mom had also died, the true compassion he heard in her voice, or the fact that she'd called him Sam. She knew who he was.

"How, uh, did you know my name?" He popped open the can's top and took a sip.

Kendall chuckled low and deep in her throat. "It's not that big of a school. I don't know your last name, if that makes you feel better." She laughed again, and Sam felt the hairs on his arms stand up. Her laughter immediately made him feel warm, safe, and happy, and yet it made him feel empty at the same time too. *Mom laughed just like that.* Sam realized. *I always loved that laugh.*

"It's Slater. My last name, that is." He stood back and held his palm up to the machine, like Vanna White with her letters on Wheel of Fortune which his Grandpa always watched. "All yours, Kendall I-don't-know-your-last-name-either."

"Kendall Richardson." She stepped forward and stuck the dollar bill that he'd just given her into the machine. The machine sucked it in and whirred. But this time, instead of spitting it out, the machine accepted the bill.

"No way!"

"Yes, really, honestly. That is my name."

"No, I mean that's just crazy. It took the dollar. How did you do that? Magic or something?"

Kendall selected bottled water and then retrieved it. She chuckled again. "Not magic. But my dad does say I have *the touch*—whatever that means. He calls me his good luck charm."

"I'll say." Sam was about to ask how her mom died, but the loud shrill of the school bell split the air.

Kendall turned and waved. "Happy birthday, Sam Slater," she said over the sound of the bell as she darted off to class.

It wasn't until Sam heard those words that he realized hers had been the only happy birthday greeting of the day aside from his grandma's.

SAM GOT THROUGH the rest of his uneventful Tuesday and was counting the minutes until the last period ended. He was sitting at a library table, his books spread before him, and was supposedly attempting to find a poem that he could use for his English paper, when he noticed Kendall walk into the room. She didn't see him. Instead her eyes were fixed on the library computer. She hurried over to it, sat down with her back to him, and then typed something. The web browser opened to eBay, and Sam thought it was odd that she'd be scanning the Internet for good deals in the middle of the school day.

Sam picked up a book of poetry, mindlessly flipping through the pages, pretending he wasn't watching her. The truth was he'd been thinking about her a lot—not in a romantic way, but because Kendall reminded him of his mom, from her little coin purse to her deep laugh. Even the way she walked. His chest constricted and his throat felt tight, as if he'd swallowed a hundred marbles.

Or maybe that wasn't it. Maybe she wasn't so much like his mom at all. Maybe his mind was just on his mom because it was his birthday. Birthdays always made him think of her more, especially this one.

What would they be doing today if Mom were still alive? Would she make his favorite cake? Would they go somewhere? Hang out on the beach? Build a campfire and listen to the waves?

Sam flipped the page again, turning the thoughts from his mind. *Don't go there, Sam. Don't do it.*

Kendall printed something off, snatched the sheet from the printer, and then rose and turned around. Her eyes scanned the room as she did, and her gaze met his.

Sam diverted his eyes and lowered his head. Then he pulled the book closer to his face, pretending to read, pretending to be fascinated by the poetry of Robert Frost.

Kendall wasn't fooled, and she approached. She pulled up the chair next to him and sat down with a flourish. "Hey you. I was going to look for you later today, and here you are." She whispered her words, leaning close, attempting to keep the librarian's wrath from falling upon them.

She laid the printout on the table, and Sam noticed it was a listing for an antique hand mirror selling for $312.

"That's interesting." He moved his eyes from the paper to her. "You know, that you wanted to talk to me." He let his voice trail off, and his stomach churned, hoping Kendall wasn't interested in anything more than friendship. He'd just split with Arielle not too long ago, and he wasn't ready to jump into another relationship. Dealing with girls in everyday life was hard enough as it was. Getting emotions involved was one hundred times worse.

"No, I don't have the hots for you, Sam. I can read the worry in your gaze." Her voice was still a whisper. Yet as he scanned her face he didn't see anger, or even romantic interest. He saw friendship, and he liked that.

"I was just thinking about your birthday and stuff." Kendall folded up the piece of paper and tucked it into her pocket. "I know how hard this day is. Personally, I'd rather skip over my birthdays completely because it never seems right celebrating them without my mom."

Sam focused on her wide, brown eyes and nodded. He was amazed she was so honest, so real.

"Yeah."

"Anyway, I'm sure your day is completely booked, but maybe later this week I can treat you to a banana split at Jenny's Creamery? As a friend only, so you don't have to worry."

Sam rubbed his chin. Then he smiled. "Okay. I think I'd like that."

"Great. I'll talk to my people and you talk to your people, and then we'll talk later and figure out a time that works."

Then, without another word, Kendall rose, patted the pocket that held her printout, and hurried out of the room.

Sam scratched his head. He didn't know what to think about Kendall, but a banana split sounded amazing.

Chapter Three

"A thief?" Mary Louise spat out the words as if her mouth were full of pepper.

Charlotte shrugged. "'Fraid so. Or at least that's what half of my family thought growing up. They say that the facts are the facts, and though it shames the family name there's nothing to be done but accept it." Charlotte sighed. "But as Anita here can tell you, there are more rumors about Elijah Coleman than there are days in the week."

"And the other half of your family, do they deny the facts?" Mary Louise leaned back in her chair and crossed her arms over her chest. It was clear from her words, and her posture, that Mary Louise believed what the paper stated: Elijah Coleman was a thief, and that was that.

"The rest of my family, well, they aren't so sure. My grandfather was born the year this incident happened. My great-grandfather Elijah—everyone called him Granddaddy—was Bedford's first postmaster. Of course, all that changed when the money, uh, disappeared. I remember being a little girl and hearing the stories."

"So what did your grandfather believe?" Hannah asked.

"My grandfather was a jovial man, but he always grew serious when anyone brought the subject up. He said he knew his father's character, and he never believed his dad stole that money."

"The money for a church—our church?" Hannah scratched her head. "I don't understand."

"Why don't you read the rest of the article?" Mary Louise interjected, flicking the paper with her fingernail.

Hannah cleared her throat and began reading. "Bedford, Nebraska, May 16. The trial of Elijah Coleman, ex-postmaster of Bedford Township, charged with the theft of funds, ended with a guilty verdict before the United States commissioner. The former postmaster was in charge of collection of the funds for the soon-to-be-built Bedford Community Church. The money went missing after the April 1 groundbreaking. Mr. Coleman's sentencing will take place Friday next."

Hannah stopped reading, and both Maxie and Mary Louise were silent. Not only that, but Charlotte noticed that some of the other women who'd been working around them had quieted too. Listening.

"So what happened?" Hannah's words were innocent enough, but they unleashed a tornado of thoughts, memories, and emotions within Charlotte.

"I don't remember all the facts clearly. But my mother told me a little bit. I do know that there was another church in town at the time, but people on this side of the valley wanted their own. They met at a barn for a while and then began praying for a church building. They felt God indeed wanted them to have a place of their own, so they started a money collection. It took them a couple of years, but they finally raised enough money." Charlotte paused. "Then my granddaddy—well, I don't know all the details, but the money disappeared. After that it took another year to raise the funds again."

"How come he was in charge of the money?" Mary Louise held her hand out, and Hannah handed her the newspaper clipping. She read it over silently, and listened for Charlotte's answer.

"I'm not sure. Maybe they didn't have a bank?" Charlotte shrugged.

"Could someone else in the community have stolen it?" Hannah asked.

"Why would anyone steal from a church?" Nancy Evans shook her head. "I can't imagine the heartbreak of those poor people."

Charlotte didn't know whom to respond to first, or what she should even say. "It would take me all day to tell you all the stories. Or rather, different versions of the same story. Sometimes—usually during family gatherings like Thanksgiving—it would come up. Some of my family is sure Granddaddy was robbed. There are others who say Granddaddy was extremely forgetful. These family members were certain he misplaced the money in his house. In fact when they tore down the old place years ago they picked over it good—sure they'd come across stashed treasure."

More women gathered around, as if Charlotte were the town crier spilling the latest news. Seeing their curious eyes on her—and noting their interest in an old family mystery—caused the muscles on the back of Charlotte's neck to tighten. It wasn't just some old fable or a fiction tale she'd heard once. This was her granddaddy, and in some way it felt like relating the story made her a traitor to her family name.

Charlotte ignored their glances and turned back to the box she was halfway through sorting. "Unfortunately, we'll never know."

"I wouldn't be so sure about that." Anita piped up. "I remember my grandmother telling me about how your granddaddy was accused. And even more than that." Anita pressed Charlotte's hand between hers. Anita's hands were warm, and her paper-thin skin felt soft, just as Charlotte's mother's had been. "Charlotte, I think I have something at home that you just might want to see. Something that might give you a few clues about the truth. Do you think you can hold out until tomorrow though? I think it will be worth the wait."

THE CHATTER OF KIDS' VOICES and the shuffling of feet bounced off the walls of Emily's sixth-period American history class.

Emily's gaze flitted past a map of the Louisiana Purchase and a poster showing Lewis and Clark on the Missouri River. Then her attention settled on the brown-haired girl sitting across the room. Andrea Zikova's eyes were focused on the paper in front of her, and her shoulder-length brown hair hung partially in front of her face. Emily wondered if Andrea—the foreign-exchange student—had seen the bulletin board Mrs. Lorenz had just put up. Black construction-paper letters stapled onto a red, white, and blue background said SPRING HISTORY PRESENTATION. Under that their teacher had posted a chart listing the student teams. Andrea and Emily were paired up. The thing was, this was the only class they had together, and Emily wasn't sure if she had even talked to Andrea all year—well, except for the one time she accidentally bumped into the girl in the cafeteria and apologized. But she had heard Andrea talking to others, and the girl was sort of hard to understand.

Where's she from? Germany? Russia? Emily couldn't remember exactly. It was something like that.

She crossed her arms across her chest, wondering if she could ask for a new partner. *It's not fair that I'm teamed up with someone who most likely knows zero about American history. I'll have to do all the work.*

And worse than that, it was a presentation. How would Andrea get up and present to everyone? Emily had a hard time understanding her. So how would they be able to work together?

Emily wondered what she should do. *I'll ask if I can switch. Surely Mrs. Lorenz will understand.* She started to go toward Mrs. Lorenz's desk, but another kid was already asking the same question.

"I'm sorry. There will be no changing partners. No exceptions," Mrs. Lorenz said, loud enough for everyone to hear.

Emily set her backpack on the seat of her desk. She glanced at Andrea and took a deep breath. *This is going to be a drag.*

Andrea got up and moved toward Emily and tapped her shoulder just as the bell rang for class to start. "Hey, I saw we are going to do the history project together."

Emily bit her lip and nodded. "Yep."

"Do you want to meet today to talk about it? Maybe after school?" She had an unusual accent.

"Um, ok, I guess." Emily hesitated.

"Okay, I will call my mom—my host mom that is. I call her mom. I dink that will be okay."

Dink? Oh. Emily realized Andrea meant *think*. "Sure. We can meet at the front of the school and walk to Mel's Place."

Behind her, Mrs. Lorenz cleared her throat, trying to get everyone's attention.

Andrea's eyes darted to the front of the room, where the history teacher was standing with a stack of papers for today's quiz.

"See you then." Emily rushed back to her desk. She pulled out a pencil and tucked the backpack under her desk, yet her mind wasn't on the quiz. Instead, she was thinking about her partner and how unfair it was that she was stuck with her.

The school day went quickly, and Emily grabbed her backpack and headed to the front door after the last bell rang. Andrea's wave and bright smile greeted her. Emily looked over her shoulder to make sure Andrea wasn't waving at someone else. When she realized she wasn't, Emily waved back.

"Hi, Andrea."

"Hey." Andrea touched her arm. "I spoke with my mom

and she needs me to hang out with my little brother, so I have to take the bus home. Can we get together Saturday? She says you can come to our house."

"Uh, sure. That will be cool."

Andrea handed Emily a piece of paper. "It is the phone number to my house." Another slight smile lifted the corners of Andrea's mouth as she hurried to the bus line.

"Okay, I guess I'll go find Sam and let him know I need a ride after all," Emily mumbled, waving to Andrea's back.

She hurried outside and pulled her hoodie over her head. The air was crisp and stung her nose. Emily tugged on her skirt as if her efforts would make it longer. She wished she had more than leggings on.

Emily spotted Sam unlocking his car.

"Hey." She hurried over to him. "I'm glad you're still here. I'm going to need a ride after all."

"Fine." He unlocked the door and tossed his backpack in the backseat. Then he climbed in, leaned across the seat, and unlocked her door. Sam seemed to be in a grumpy mood, but Emily didn't say anything. Mentioning it to Sam only made it worse.

"So have you ever talked to that girl Andrea Zikova?" Emily slid in and slammed the door.

"Who?" Sam adjusted his mirror and then paused with his hand halfway to the ignition.

"You know, that foreign-exchange student. We're doing a project together for American history."

"Oh yeah, a few times. She's in my math class, even though she's not supposed to be in twelfth grade." He smirked. "I think she has the best grade. Maybe there's something in that European water that makes kids over there so smart. In San Diego the exchange students were always the smartest too." He started the car, but his eyes weren't focused on the dashboard or on Emily. Instead, he was focused on his rearview mirror.

"Yeah, I wish I could talk in another language like that. It must have taken her a long time to learn English though," Emily said.

"Duh, it's only Americans who have a hard time learning a second language." Sam opened the door and shut off the car. "Hold on, I'll be right back."

"Where are you going?" She called after him. He didn't pause. She turned in her seat and noticed a small yellow Volkswagen parked behind Sam's car. A pretty girl was in the driver's seat. Sam waved, and she motioned to the passenger seat. He flipped his hair, showed off a broad smile, and then climbed in.

Emily had seen that girl before, but she'd never talked to her. She thought her name was Kennedy or Keith or some other weird boy name. Emily had never seen her hanging around with Sam's usual friends. The girl always looked kind of suspect, like she was hiding something, or as if she didn't feel anyone else was worthy to hang out with her.

Emily could see them chatting about something. The girl laughed and tossed her head back. Her black hair perfectly framed her pixie face and swished as she talked to Sam.

Then, as if feeling Emily's eyes on her, the girl turned her head, locked onto Emily's gaze—and winked.

Emily felt heat rising to her cheeks, and she quickly

turned back around to face the dashboard of the car. Anger gurgled in Emily's chest like Grandma's coffeepot in the morning. She didn't know what made her madder, the fact that the girl had watched her watching and mocked her or that Sam was hanging out with another girl. He and Arielle had just broken up. Who did he think he was? It's not like he was some heartthrob like Tom Holland or anything.

A few minutes later Sam climbed back in the car. She resisted the urge to turn and watch the girl drive away.

"You could have left the car running." Emily crossed her arms over her chest and pulled them tight to her. "It's freezing in here."

"I wasn't gone that long, Emily. Don't be a baby."

"Whatever."

Sam started the car, and Emily pointed the heating vent in her direction.

"You have to wait until the engine heats up. It's just blowing cold air."

"I know. I'm not stupid." Emily closed the vents and then locked her eyes on Sam. "So what were you doing with Kendrick?"

"It's Kendall. And it's none of your business."

"But you just broke up with Arielle."

"Tell me something I don't know."

"Do you like her?"

"No, Emily." He tapped the flat of his hand against the steering wheel. "I always hang out with people I absolutely hate."

She sat silent most of the way home and thought about what it would be like to be an exchange student in another country. Emily tried to imagine traveling across the world, being away from her family, and going to a school where they spoke another language. The thought scared her, and a wave of loneliness washed over her as she remembered her first few months in Bedford.

"Have you talked to Andrea much?" Emily asked, trying to steer the conversation back to something that wouldn't make Sam so mad. "I was talking to her today, and she was talking about her host mom. She just calls her mom. I don't think it's right."

"Why not?" Sam tapped his fingers on the steering wheel.

"It's just weird. I think it would make her real mom mad, don't you? I don't think I could call someone I didn't know mom or dad."

"Yeah, what about our dad?"

"But he *is* my dad."

"You didn't know him when he came. You still don't very much."

"That's different."

Sam nodded, but didn't continue down that path. "So what's your project on?"

"On the railroad coming into Nebraska. You know, how it affected settlement and stuff."

"Sounds boring."

"Ha, thanks. It will be cool, I suppose. Maybe Grandma knows about it."

"Gee, Emily, she's not that old."

Emily chose to ignore that comment and Sam's sour attitude.

"I'm going over Andrea's house on Saturday."

Sam's head flipped around. "You're going over to the Cunninghams' house? No thanks."

She felt the skin on her arms grow cold, even colder than it had been when she had the air blowing on her.

"Andrea lives with the Cunninghams? They're her host parents?"

"Yeah, didn't you know that?"

This can't be happening to me. First I'm going to do all the work. Second I'm going to have to be tortured as I do it. Emily moaned. "Poor thing. To have a mom like Mrs. Cunningham who always has to put her nose in everyone else's business. And then there's Lily . . ."

"I overheard Andrea saying they share a room. Maybe they'll ask you to spend the night." A spurt of laughter burst from Sam's lips.

"Haha, very funny." She playfully slugged Sam's arm.

Their car passed Bedford Community Church, and Emily was surprised to see so many cars there this late in the day.

"Is there a church party we didn't get invited to?" Emily asked, looking closer.

"Gee, a party. A celebration. What a concept."

Sam turned his head and eyed the church as they went by.

"I'm not sure, but is Grandma's car there? Did you see it?"

"I think I did. Bummer. There's no cookies and milk waiting for us on the table. I thought today was just like any other day," he smirked. "I was wrong. It's even worse."

Emily ignored Sam's comment. And his pouting. Then it hit her, and she held in a smile. *Sam thinks we forgot his birthday*. She didn't want to interrupt his sour mood to tell him that there was going to be a party with at least two presents. She'd helped Christopher wrap one yesterday. She'd made and wrapped something too.

"I hope everything is all right at the church." Emily pulled her cell phone from her bag and thought about calling home. Then again she doubted Grandpa would answer, or Christopher either.

"Everything's fine. Don't worry your pretty little head about Grandma; you have enough to worry about."

"Yeah, like what?"

"Like what to pack for the sleepover."

"You're so funny." Emily sunk lower in her seat. "What am I going to do?"

"I'm just teasing you. You don't have to deal with Lily. It's Andrea you're working with, and—"

The chirping tune of Emily's cell phone interrupted Sam's words. Emily fumbled with her phone, trying to answer it. Finally she answered just before it went to voice mail. "Hello."

"Hi, Emily. This is Andrea, from school." As if Emily didn't recognize her voice.

"Oh, hi."

"I got your number from Ashley. I hope that is fine."

"Yes, uh, not a problem."

Sam looked at Emily, confused.

Andrea, she mouthed.

"I talked with my sister and her partner was given twice. Mrs. Lorenz says she should be in our project. The good news is there will be now three."

"Three?" Emily's eyes widened. *Lily*. "Are you sure? I mean I can find someone else. Maybe you should just be with your sister. It might be easier..."

"Oh, no. I would not think of that. Maybe on Saturday you could spend the night."

"Uh," Emily cast a desperate glance at Sam, who was cracking up. "Okay. Sure."

Andrea let out a squeal, said good-bye, and hung up.

Emily looked at the phone in her hand.

Sam turned onto the dirt road leading to Heather Creek. "Let me guess. You have a new partner?"

Emily didn't answer. She just jammed the phone into her pocket, covered her face with her hands, and moaned.

Chapter Four

As the day wore on, the women of the church continued working, nourished by the leftovers in the kitchen and by each other's conversations. Yet what should have been a delightful time of reconnecting with friends after a long winter had transformed into an awkward afternoon. Not only had all the dust and mildew of boxes that had been sitting for decades given Charlotte a headache, but something was also wrong with the women —or rather, with their interaction with her.

Charlotte looked again at the faces around her. She'd known these women her whole life. She'd gone to church with them, had attended Bible study with them. She'd held Mary Louise's hand when she learned her mother had cancer. She had often walked the county fair with Maxie. And now their friendship was transforming with the marriage of Pete and Dana. Maxie would now be family. Yet she felt that the tone of the day had changed, and it was as if *she*, not her granddaddy, had been accused of stealing funds from the church.

After Hannah showed her the news article about Elijah Coleman, Charlotte had attempted to get back to work as if nothing had happened. But the truth was, everything had changed.

Hannah approached her with a sympathetic look. "Charlotte, it's getting late. Don't you need to get home? Isn't today Sam's birthday?"

"Yes, we're having a family dinner. Bill's family, Dana, and Rosemary are coming over." Charlotte glanced at her watch, and her eyes widened. "Four o'clock already?" She brushed her hands off on her pants. "I can't believe I've been looking through these boxes for so long. But I've found some interesting things, you know, for the display." She forced a smile and waved a hand to her "display" pile.

Hannah's furrowed brow told her she was seeing through the charade. "Do you think you'll find anything more about your great-grandfather?"

"Besides more accusations? I doubt it, but I'm hopeful." Charlotte wished that Anita would have given her at least a hint of whatever information she had. It didn't seem fair to have to wait another day, trying to pretend that nothing was wrong. And this wasn't the first time the scandal of her Granddaddy had ruined Charlotte's day.

Charlotte's mind took her back to the week before her own wedding. Opal, her mother, had taken Charlotte to her old cedar trunk, showing her family and wedding photos of her and her husband, William, Charlotte's dad. It was the passing of the torch, so to speak, a history of their family and its traditions. Yet when they'd come across similar news clippings about Elijah Coleman, dark clouds had descended upon that bright day too. How could one man, long dead, continue to stir so many questions?

Charlotte rose from the folding chair. A pain shot up her back and down her leg, evidence of the hours she'd sat there sorting.

Hannah lifted Charlotte's coat from the back of her chair and handed it to her. "You know, you've done more work in one day than I expected anyone to do. You've put in your fair share. Don't worry about digging through this old stuff anymore."

"Are you kidding? I'll be back tomorrow and the day after too." Charlotte's voice rose an octave, and all eyes in the room turned in her direction. "As a matter of fact, I'm going to find out the truth about my great-grandfather and his dealings. It needs to come out in the open. The truth is the truth, and hiding it—"

"The truth is that he's innocent." Anita interrupted. Then she used her cane to help her stand. The old woman's cheeks were brushed with rouge and powder, but she wore no smile. Anita straightened her shoulders.

All eyes turned her direction.

"And Anita Wilson, how would you know that?" Mary Louise spouted.

"I know it 'cause my mama told me. Also, I have evidence back home.... something I'll share *privately* with Charlotte. I was going to wait until tomorrow, but I can see I need to say something now." She jutted out her chin. "What the newspaper doesn't say is that Elijah Coleman was accused by the state, but not by the church members of Bedford. In fact, the men of the church..." Anita's eyes welled up with tears. "They believed in him so much they went in and asked to serve time with him. It's said that so many men filled up that lone jail cell that the judge dropped the whole thing—no farming was getting done. The general store was closed. No one was there to meet the train."

Charlotte covered her mouth with her hand. "Really?" Her throat felt tight. "I wonder why my mother didn't tell me."

"Why, your mama wasn't there. Your grandmother either. They weren't even born. My guess is, since the mystery was never solved your grandfather didn't want to bring it up." Anita smiled. "Sometimes it's easier just to treasure the truth in your heart than try to explain it."

Charlotte finished buttoning up her coat, and then she moved to Anita's side. "Can I walk you to your car?"

"I'm getting a ride with Nancy, but I'd like that."

Charlotte extended her arm, and Anita slipped her own arm around it, using Charlotte to help her balance.

"Hope you can make it tomorrow, Charlotte." Mary Louise's voice rang out like a church bell over the prairie.

"I'll be here. You can count on it," Charlotte assured her. "You better believe I'm not only going to find the facts. I'm also gonna prove that my great-granddaddy is innocent and do a spring cleaning on my family's name."

CHARLOTTE COULDN'T HELP but notice Sam was especially quiet as he ate his piece of birthday cake after dinner that evening.

Sam, Charlotte, Bob, Bill, and Pete sat at the table while the other family members sat in the family room eating their cake. Rosemary hadn't arrived for dinner, and Charlotte was starting to worry about her. The phone had been busy when she tried calling earlier, so maybe she was just held up at home.

Sam had been quieter over the last few days, and Charlotte was reminded of last February, when he'd run away to find his father. So much had happened since then.

Thank You, Lord, for being with us through it all. Now please be with Sam as he considers his future. So much, she knew, depended on the choices he made now.

"Is it good, Sam?" she asked, pouring more milk into his glass. "I used your mom's recipe."

"Yeah." He nodded. "It's good, Grandma. It tastes just like hers."

"It's a very special day, Sam. I'm sure your mom would be proud of you. We are." Charlotte looked toward Bob, hoping he'd join in.

Bob winked at her, getting the hint.

"Yes, Sam, like your grandmother said, you've done a lot of growing up. And I guess you're officially a man now."

Pete chuckled and waved his hand toward Sam. "Um, yeah, Sam, you're a man, which means starting tomorrow you're taking over all my chores, and I'm retiring."

Laughter filled the room, and Charlotte was glad when Sam played along, giving a shocked expression. "Do I *have* to be responsible? Actually, Uncle Pete, if it comes with more chores, I think I'll pass. I don't mind being seventeen again."

"If only it could work that way." Bill patted his gut. "I'd still be twenty-one and able to jog a mile without having to stop and catch my breath."

Bob pulled an envelope from his shirt pocket. "Well, since you've decided not to have a birthday I'll keep this." Bob waved the envelope in the air.

Charlotte had tried to talk Bob into something typical—a nice card, a few presents—but Bob said that those things were kid stuff.

As Sam eyed the envelope, his mouth slid into a lopsided grin. "Well, in that case."

Bob slid the envelope across the table.

"Wait, Grandpa," Christopher interrupted. "He can't open that until we give him our stuff first." Christopher grabbed the box on the table wrapped in Sunday comics and handed it to Sam.

"Thanks, Christopher. I love the comics." Sam held the box up and began reading, chuckling to himself. Then Sam shook it around and listened to the rattling. "Is it a puzzle? Or maybe a box of rocks?"

Christopher wagged a finger at him. "Are you trying to drive me crazy or something?"

"Okay, fine, I'll open it."

Sam opened the box and peered inside. Then he reached down and pulled out a candy bar.

"There are eighteen of them." Christopher smiled. "And I promise I won't sneak into your room and eat any."

"Thanks, little man." Sam patted Christopher's head.

"Okay, my turn." Emily handed Sam a box that was smaller than Christopher's. "I hope you like it. I sort of made it myself."

Sam opened the box and found a T-shirt folded into a square inside.

"You made the shirt?" Sam asked.

"Well, no, but I designed the front."

Sam unfolded it and laughter burst from his lips. "'Procrastinators Unite . . . Tomorrow.' I like that!"

"One more," Anna piped up. "We weren't sure what to get you, but I hope you like this."

Sam opened a small envelope and pulled out a gift card for a skate shop in Harding. "Wow, very cool."

"We figured you'd find something there," Bill added.

Sam put the gift card with the other items, and then he looked at the envelope.

"Go ahead," Charlotte urged him.

Sam's expression grew serious as he opened it. His eyes widened when he saw the numbers on the check.

"Whoa, Grandpa. No, you can't do this."

"It's for your future—for college, I hope." Bob leaned back in his chair.

Sam nodded, and Charlotte saw his shoulders deflate slightly.

"Want to play checkers, Grandpa?" Christopher asked, realizing the celebration was over.

"Sure, set it up." Bob turned his attention to Christopher.

Sam glanced around the room. He looked down at his small pile of gifts.

See, I told you he's not too old for presents, wrapping paper, and party games, Charlotte wanted to say.

She reached across the table and patted his hand. "I know a college fund isn't as much fun as a pile of gifts to unwrap or a custom paint job for your car, but you'll thank us someday. I promise."

Sam nodded. "Oh, don't worry, Grandma. I thank you

now. Thanks. This is amazing." He stood. "And I hate to do this, but do you mind if I head out? I told Jake and Paul I'd meet them for burgers at Mel's. They wanted to celebrate my birthday."

"But you just had dinner." Charlotte's jaw dropped. "And cake."

"Yeah, but you know guys need two dinners." Pete smiled.

Charlotte glanced at the clock. It was almost 8:00 PM and a school night. More than that, it was already dark. *Still, he's eighteen now.* Charlotte had learned with Denise that being too restrictive only caused rebellion. She forced a smile. "Okay. Have fun. Just don't stay out too late."

"Cool." Sam hurried toward the door and grabbed his jacket. "Thanks, everyone."

Anna approached Charlotte holding baby Will, who was now sleeping, and smiled. "I can't believe Sam's old enough to head out alone, and meet up with friends in a restaurant, not to mention go to college soon. I remember getting photos in Denise's Christmas cards of a chubby-cheeked little boy. He's anything but little now."

"Time marches on. I know that well. I've been sifting through it."

"What do you mean, Charlotte?" Anna asked, holding Will out to her. "Do you want to hold him?"

"Of course. You know you don't have to ask." Charlotte snuggled the baby on her lap inside a blue fleece blanket.

Anna quietly cleared the cake dishes as Emily headed upstairs, followed by Madison and Jennifer. Charlotte had no doubt all three would emerge in twenty minutes with nails painted in various shades of pink.

"Yes, I sifted through history all right. Today the Women's Group started cleaning out the church basement. There were all sorts of things—old bulletins, photos, cookbooks. Piles of Sunday school materials that went back years." She stroked Will's cheek and then turned to her older son. "Bill, someone found a photo of you when you were baptized, and I think I recognized at least one rodeo drawing in the front of an old hymnal. Pete, you even practiced writing your name on some of them. For years you didn't understand that when you ran out of scratch paper you had to stop drawing." She glanced over at Pete, who shrugged.

"There's something else. Remember that story I told you about your great-great-grandfather—I call him Granddaddy—and the situation with Bedford Community Church?" Charlotte asked, attempting to make her tone as lighthearted as possible.

"Yeah, I remember Uncle Chet talking about that before." Bill cut himself a second helping of cake.

Anna took a sip from her cocoa. "I don't think I remember hearing about it." She playfully punched Bill's arm. "Are you trying to keep family secrets from me?"

Bill's jaw dropped. "I told you, remember? My great-great-grandfather stole money from the church and then got arrested for it."

"You don't have to put it so bluntly. This is your mother's family we're talking about," Bob stated. Then he glanced at Christopher from across the table. "King me."

"Ahh, Grandpa." Christopher added another red checker on top of his grandpa's piece. "I don't remember the story.

We have a thief in our family? Like Jesse James or something? That's cool."

Anna straightened in her seat. "It's not cool, Christopher. Stealing is a crime against society. More than that, it's against God."

"And it's not at all like Jesse James," Charlotte butted in. "No one is sure what happened. I mean, there are a lot of theories. It's possible Granddaddy just lost the money. Or that someone robbed him."

Bill wiped his face as if trying to hide a smirk. "And what's so important about bringing this up tonight?"

For the next ten minutes Charlotte told them about the church's upcoming open house and history display. She also told them about the clipping Hannah found in one of the boxes.

"Sounds like someone found an excuse for cleaning out the basement," Bob mumbled under his breath.

"We started talking about it today, and Anita Wilson says she has something that might be able to help me—something that could assist in proving that Elijah was innocent after all."

"Listen to you." Bill waved a hand her direction. "You talk as if you know the guy. It's an interesting story and all, but it's not like figuring out what happened—or even making an educated guess—will make a difference."

"He's right, Char," Bob jumped in. "Personally, I just think Mrs. Wilson is a little lonely and is looking for company."

"Yeah, too bad that Elijah Granddaddy guy wasn't Jesse James." Christopher scratched his head. "Ha! King *me*, Grandpa!"

The baby shifted softly in her arms, and Charlotte ran a hand over his feather-soft hair. *Maybe they're right. Maybe it's all just a waste of time.*

"I don't know. I have to disagree," Dana interrupted. "I think it's fascinating and very worthy. I mean, five or ten years from now people like Mrs. Wilson won't be around. If we don't take time to listen to their stories now, it'll be too late."

"Good point." Charlotte pointed her finger in the air and chuckled. "I'll have to remember that."

Anna gathered up all the napkins and mugs as the conversation wound down.

"Mommy, Mommy! Look! Look! Emily painted our nails." The stomping of very unladylike feet pounded down the stairs. Jennifer and Madison hurried into the room, flapping their small hands. Even Anna couldn't help but smile at their excitement, despite the fact they'd forgotten their manners.

"Wow, look at that. How pretty," Anna said, even though it was impossible to actually see anything with all the girls' excited movement. She placed a finger over her lips. "Now, shhh, girls. Calm down for a second. You interrupted while Grandma was just about to say something."

Charlotte searched her mind, trying to remember what she had been planning to say, but it was gone. Then seeing Jennifer's round chin with the slightest dimple, just like her father's, reminded her.

"Oh yes. I was just going to say I think Dana's right. The story of Elijah Coleman matters because it's our story. It's part of all of us. Whether past or present, family is family, and we need to do what we can to support each other."

As they sat there, a knock sounded at the door.

"I'll get it." Anna hurried to open it, and as she did they were greeted with Rosemary's red cheeks and chipper greeting.

"Happy birthday, Sam," she chirped as she entered.

"Rosemary." Charlotte stood, cradling the baby close to her so they didn't wake him. "I was wondering where you were. I'm so sorry, but Sam headed out not too long ago. He was going out to dinner with friends."

"Oh, I'm sorry I missed him." She placed her wrapped present on the table. "I got out of the shop late today. And then I got home and was just headed out the door again when the phone rang. It was my friend from Harding—you know, the one who owns the antique shop." Rosemary took her coat off and then rubbed her hands together, warming them.

"Oh, yes, Margaret, isn't it? I think you've introduced me before."

"Yes, that's right. It was Margaret." Rosemary hurried to the table, cut herself a piece of cake, and sat down. "I have to admit, what she had to say has me flustered. She was telling me about a strange man who came into her store with a young woman who he said was his daughter. He had some old silver jewelry he was trying to sell. Margaret said the jewelry was beautiful, but she thought for sure that it was stolen."

As she spoke, Charlotte felt a pain in her chest. She didn't want to keep listening to what else Rosemary had to say, but Rosemary took a deep breath and then continued.

"The man and girl said they were from Bedford, and Margaret wanted to know if I knew them. Then I remembered the girl. She'd been in my store before. She asked for store credit, but I had to decline her. I wouldn't have thought much of it, but she was wearing a beautiful necklace—one I was sure was an antique. Also . . ." Rosemary turned to Charlotte. "I remembered the girl again because I saw her today. I was picking out a birthday card, and she was too. We chatted for a while, and we soon figured out she was also picking out a birthday card for Sam. I didn't realize they knew each other. I just thought you should know, Charlotte. Don't mention it now, but in the future it might be something you should talk to Sam about. The last thing he needs is to get wrapped up in trouble."

"Thanks for letting me know." Charlotte turned to Bob. "We'll keep our eyes and ears open. So far, Sam hasn't gotten into big trouble or hung around people who have, but it's something to watch for."

SAM ENTERED MEL'S, and the scent of food made him smile even though he wasn't hungry. He'd find something small to eat. It was the least he could do. After all, he wasn't buying.

He scanned the room and his eyes met Kendall's. "Hey there." He waved to her and hurried over to where she sat. "Thanks for inviting me."

"Yeah, no problem. I'm glad I caught you in the school parking lot. I talked to Paul and Jake, and they'll meet us at Jenny's Creamery when we go for our banana splits." She opened the menu and spread it in front of him. "So now, Sam, what would you like? I'm thinking of the rib platter."

Sam nodded. "You didn't seem like the salad type." He closed the menu. "Sounds good. I'm going to have a club sandwich and fries, and then I'd love to know what you were doing on eBay. Were you buying or selling?"

Kendall turned and eyed him for a moment, as if trying to see if he could be trusted. Finally her questioning glance transformed into a smile. "I don't ever, ever share the stuff that I'm going to tell you; the information is valuable, very valuable. But I like you, Sam. I think we're connected, you and me. So if you promise not to tell another soul, then I'll let you in on our secret. My and my dad's secret, that is."

Chapter Five

Charlotte parked in front of Anita's small house, amazed by how little it had changed since she was a young girl and had visited there with her mother.

Last night she'd had a hard time sleeping. First, Sam's birthday and sifting through the layers of church history had made her ponder how quickly life seemed to pass. One day you were living it. The next your name was just something jotted inside the cover of a family Bible.

Second, she wondered what Anita had wanted to tell her, or was it *show* her? Charlotte had known Anita a long time, and it seemed strange that the woman would be so insistent about having information that Charlotte would want about Elijah Coleman. If she had information, why did she wait until now? How come she hadn't shown Charlotte months, or even years ago?

Charlotte climbed from her warm car into the cold morning, her breath evident in the air.

The pinkish-brown paint was chipping, and the walkway out front hadn't been cleared of last week's snow, which had hardened, making it difficult to walk on. *I wonder how Anita managed with her bad ankle.*

Even though the rose bushes in front of the house were bare and had been pruned close to the ground, in her mind's eye Charlotte pictured how they had looked in July, colorful and heavy with buds.

She knocked at the door but didn't wait for Anita to answer. Charlotte stepped inside, thankful for the warmth that enveloped her, and called out merrily, "Anyone home?"

"In here, sweetie. Just pouring us some tea."

The living room had navy blue carpet. It was thirty years old but looked as new as the day it was installed. Throw pillows were perfectly arranged on the couch, and the television, its sound muted, was tuned to the cooking channel.

Charlotte kicked off her shoes and lined them up next to Anita's rain boots by the front door. "I smell scones." She breathed in the scent of fresh-from-the-oven pastries. "Are they cinnamon?" she called.

"Of course they're cinnamon. When have you ever visited that I haven't made them for you?"

Charlotte padded across the carpet, suddenly feeling like a child again. As she entered the kitchen, longing for her mother swept over her—deeper than she'd experienced in years.

"Hi there." Charlotte pulled Anita into a hug. "Thanks for inviting me over."

"Yes, well, I'm glad you were able to get away. I know things are busy with the kids."

Charlotte shrugged. "Of course, but they're a blessing; they really are."

She noticed an old shoe box on the table with a purple ribbon tied around it. Charlotte guessed that it had something to do with Granddaddy. Yet she also knew that the topic would only come up after she'd had a cup of tea and a scone and had filled Anita in on all the family news. Still, the question wouldn't leave her. . . . *Why had Anita waited until now?*

"English breakfast tea okay?" Anita poured a cup for Charlotte even as she asked. Then she poured one for herself.

Anita settled into her chair with the slightest moan. "These old bones aren't what they used to be."

"Are you kidding? I think you're doing great. It's so wonderful to see you up and around."

Anita waved a hand in the air. She took a sip from her teacup and then focused on Charlotte's gaze. "So tell me about the kids and about the wedding. Are you up to your neck in plans, or is Dana's family taking care of all of it?"

For the next thirty minutes Charlotte shared everything she could about the wedding, about the recent fire on their farm, about her newest grandson, and the 101 things the teens were up to.

"I can't believe Sam will be graduating. My, time does fly."

"Does it ever." Anita added more cream to her now-tepid tea. "Speaking of time, I have something to show you."

With shaky, age-spotted hands, Anita untied the ribbon from the box. Charlotte looked inside to see a stack of envelopes.

"Are those letters? Who are they from?"

"They're letters all right, from my grandmother's identical twin sister in Boston. They wrote each other every month, at least once."

Charlotte picked up a letter, amazed by how fragile the paper seemed—and by how perfect the penmanship was.

"Miss Wilma Banks. Bedford, Nebraska," Charlotte read. It was postmarked 1879.

"No need for more of an address than that. There were just a few hundred folks in town at the time."

"May I read it?"

"Of course. Read them all, if they interest you. But I sorted them. I think you'll want to read the ones on top first. They're the important ones. They're the ones that talk about Elijah Coleman and the missing money."

Moisture blurred Charlotte's vision as she opened the first envelope. Somehow a sense of rightness suddenly filled the room. It was as if she was supposed to be here at this moment, and in a strange way it seemed as if all these letters had been saved just for her.

She unfolded the sheet of paper, but before she read she patted Anita's hand. "It's strange for me sometimes to think of my ancestors as real people. They're names in the family Bible and old photographs, but it's hard to picture them as being real."

"Oh, they were real people all right, and quite the characters too. Your mother, Opal, and I were born just a month apart and attended school together all the way through. I knew your grandmother well. And I met your great-grandmother a few times. She was a quiet soul. She kept to herself a lot, but a few times I got a glimpse of her real personality. She was a singer in the old days. I heard she used to be very outgoing. But, well, the truth is, the problems with the church's money changed things. Even though most of the church stood behind Elijah and Lavina, believing that Elijah didn't steal it, the stigma of the event stayed with them throughout their lives. Everybody knew everything, and even if he didn't steal, he was careless. And the church suffered because of it. Quite a mess."

"Do you think the letters have the answers?"

"Maybe not the answers, but clues at least. Like I said, those five on top are the most interesting. They focus on the weeks prior to and after the events. They are my great-aunt's letters, remember, so she was just responding to whatever news my grandmother sent." Anita sighed and rubbed her temple; Charlotte could tell the excitement and work of entertaining a visitor was wearing on her.

"I understand. Do you mind if I take these letters home? I don't want to wear you out."

"Good idea. My recliner is calling me. And after that, an old Cary Grant movie." Anita offered a closed-lipped, contented smile. "That's what I call a good day."

Charlotte rose, returned the lid to the shoe box, and retied the ribbon. Eagerness percolated in her chest. She couldn't wait to get home and settle in with these letters. "Anita, is it okay if I ask you something?" Charlotte tried to make her voice sound casual as she carried her teacup and saucer across the room, setting them gently inside the porcelain sink.

"Yes, of course. What is it?"

"Well, I was wondering why you waited so long to give me these letters. You knew my parents my whole life. Didn't you ever think of passing the information on to my father about Granddaddy? Or bringing the letters over to me after their passing?"

Anita smiled. "Yes, of course. I would have if I'd known about them. You see, when I broke my ankle and could hardly move or get out of bed, I finally had time to go through my mother's old cedar trunk. I'd been meaning to do it for years. I just told myself, 'After my to-do list is done, I'll do it.' As we all know, the to-do list is never done."

"So you found the letters in the trunk?"

"Yes, and when I read about Elijah Coleman I had it on my list to call you." A soft chuckle bubbled from her lips. "See, it's the fault of my to-do list yet again."

"Oh, I understand. Believe me." Charlotte's own list rolled through her mind as soon as she said it, but she quickly pushed it away.

"When the story of Elijah Coleman came up yesterday, I remembered the letters. I'm so glad you were there where I could see you and ask you to come over. Otherwise, dear, who knows how many more months would have passed before I'd finally gotten them into your hands."

Charlotte offered Anita a gentle hug as she headed out. "Well, thank you so much for these."

"Yes, I'm just glad I found the letters while I was still walking this earth. No one else going through my things would know the connection. I'd say the information is pretty interesting. And maybe you'll come to the same conclusion that I did—that Elijah Coleman could not have stolen that money."

Anita's words stayed with Charlotte as she carefully watched her footing on the icy walkway. They stayed with her as she drove home. It was strange how just a few days ago she hadn't given her great-grandparents much thought at all—and now their story was taking up so much of her time.

She looked at the brick buildings as she drove through town, trying to imagine Bedford 130 years ago. People had lived in community together, supporting each other just like they did today.

"And just like they'll be doing fifty years from now," Charlotte mumbled to herself. Somehow it made her life—her story—matter so much more.

She was still making her way home when an old yellow Volkswagen drove by in the other direction. Charlotte paused when she noticed Sam in the passenger's seat. Their eyes met for the slightest moment before the car continued down the road.

"Sam Slater, whatever are you doing away from school in the middle of a school day?" she wondered aloud.

Charlotte scoured her mind for any memory of the Volkswagen—or, more specifically, that girl who was driving it.

Chapter Six

Emily held her lunch tray carefully. The smell of her veggie burger making her stomach growl. The line shuffled forward slowly, and she wished it would go faster so she could find a place to sit and eat, and then get out of there. With Ashley absent, lunchtime wasn't fun. There were so many social circles that didn't like the intrusion of a new person. It was better to just eat and go as quickly as possible.

She couldn't believe Ashley had missed school to go shopping in Harding with her mom. Emily knew her grandma would have never allowed that. Well, maybe she would if she had gone through all the cancer stuff that Mrs. Givens had gone through. Facing your own possible death seemed to have an effect on some people, making them reconsider what really mattered. Emily supposed school wasn't one of those things—or at least it wasn't as high up the list as a mother-and-daughter shopping trip. That idea sobered Emily as she thought about all the times with her mom that she was missing. She suddenly wished she didn't have to eat—didn't have to try to put on a happy face in the middle of all these noisy kids.

Emily was waiting in line to get a salad when she heard a familiar voice behind her.

"Seriously, Lily, if you're going to cheat from my history test, at least don't copy *all* the answers," spouted Nicole Evans.

"But I didn't..." Lily's voice started and then stopped. "Whatever."

"You almost made me get detention," Nicole continued. "Could you imagine what my dad would do? I wouldn't get the car this weekend. And who else would you get to drive you around? You'd be stuck at home with your dear, sweet, foreign sister." Her words were sharp, and Emily couldn't believe her ears. *How could Nicole speak so cruelly to her friend?*

Emily glanced over her shoulder and noticed Lily's downcast eyes. Then she quickly looked away. She scanned the cafeteria and spotted Hunter across the room hanging out with some of his rodeo friends. She was considering heading over there when someone else caught her attention. It was Andrea, sitting against the far wall. Alone.

She wasn't looking around or interacting with anyone else. Instead she just sat there, slightly slumped over, focused on her lunch. Suddenly, Emily realized she and Andrea might have something in common.

Emily walked in her direction. "Hey there."

Andrea jumped slightly and looked up. Her eyes widened with surprise. Then before Emily could blink, a smile spread across Andrea's face.

"Hi, Em-i-ly." Andrea patted the seat beside her.

Emily smiled, actually liking the way Andrea said her name in three distinct syllables.

They sat silently for a few seconds, and Emily tried to think of something to say.

"I was thinking it might be good to go to the library to find books for our project. That might work better. You know, instead of a sleepover."

"Or we could do both." Andrea's face glowed. "Tomorrow library and Saturday sleeping at my house."

Emily bit her lip and nodded. "Yeah, about that. Did you, uh, mention it to Lily?"

"Not yet, but I talked to my mom, and she says it will be good."

Emily nodded, took a bite of her carrot stick, and swallowed. "Is that weird, you know, calling Mrs. Cunningham *Mom*?"

Andrea shrugged. "It was at first, but my exchange coordinator says it is a good idea. It helps me to connect more with my family." Andrea tucked her hair behind her ear. "It is fun, you know, to have a sister. Back home I only have one younger brudder."

Emily was getting used to the way Andrea said "brother." In fact she noticed that most of the time Andrea didn't pronounce her *th*'s.

The sound of girls' laughter carried across the cafeteria, and Andrea's gaze followed it. Emily looked too and noticed that Lily was sitting on the other side of the cafeteria with Nicole Evans and some of their other friends. Emily looked at Andrea and saw the slightest tinge of sadness in her gaze. Then Andrea blinked, and the look was gone, like a windshield wiper brushing off the rain.

Emily wanted to ask why Lily wasn't sitting with her "sister," but she didn't want to make her feel bad.

Emily took a sip from her chocolate milk. "So, what's it like, you know, living at the Cunningham house?"

Andrea took a large bite from her burger, and Emily wasn't sure if she had heard her. Or maybe Andrea was just trying to ignore the question.

Then she swallowed and turned to Emily. "It is good, you know. It is not like home. I share a room with Lily, which is hard and good."

"What do you mean?" Emily heard Nicole's laughter again and felt her neck muscles tense.

"It is hard because Lily has had her own room her whole life. Sometimes she does not like it when my things are on her side of the room." Andrea giggled. "Although my side seems to shrink every week."

Emily took a bite of her veggie burger, waiting for Andrea to tell her the good part, although she couldn't imagine what that could be.

"It is good, too, because we often talk at night. Both of us are night owls—I think that is how you say it—and we talk even after everyone else is asleep."

"Really? What do you talk about?"

Andrea shrugged. "School, friends, boys—well, at least on most nights. On weekends Lily goes with Nicole a lot."

"And don't you go with her? That seems sort of weird, leaving you home."

"I know." Andrea lowered her gaze to her lap. "I suppose it is fine. I spend time with Mom or I talk to my friends back home on Skype. I guess Lily made a deal with Mom that she is not my babysitter. Nicole told me that. She . . ." Andrea's voice trailed off. "Mom also said it was her idea to have an exchange student, not Lily's." Andrea sighed. "And really it's easier when Lily is not there, so I do not mind that much."

Emily finished her burger, wondering how she should respond to that. She was glad Andrea was being truthful, and she wished there were something she could do to help. And even though she didn't say anything, she hoped that Lily would be away with Nicole when she stayed the night. Lily might be forced to be nice to Andrea, but she wasn't sure if that would go for her too. A shiver trailed up Emily's arms, just imagining what it would be like trying to get along with Lily for a whole night.

"You're from Czechoslovakia, right?" Emily asked, changing the subject. "I think that's what I remember hearing."

"Well, it used to be called that when our country was joined with Slovakia. In 1993 we got our independence and we're our own country again—the Czech Republic."

"So do you miss any food, you know, from back home?"

"Oh yes! My mother makes wonderful dumplings and goulash. We also have carp for dinner on Christmas. I didn't think I liked it very much until I missed it this year."

"Carp? Like fish?"

Andrea turned in her seat, and her face brightened. "Yes, every Christmas Eve men have fish in huge barrels that they sell on the street. We get one and keep it in the bathtub and then—"

"Wait, wait, wait. The fish is *alive*?"

Andrea nodded.

"And big?"

Andrea spread her hands about two feet.

"And you keep it in your *bathtub?* That's weird."

Andrea's face fell slightly. "Not weird, just different. Everyone does it."

"Oh, you know, you're right. Not weird, just different. *Very* different."

For the next few minutes Andrea talked about her family's apartment in some town whose name Emily couldn't pronounce. She also talked about her school and the mall she and her friend used to go to every Saturday.

"I bet you think Bedford is like going back in time. I imagine you think it's *different* we don't have a mall—or any decent shopping."

"No, that's just weird. *Very* weird." Andrea chuckled.

By the time the bell rang, signaling that lunch was over, Emily was already thinking about things around Bedford that Andrea might appreciate—like learning to bake a pie with Grandma or riding on Uncle Pete's tractor. Emily assumed that since the Cunninghams lived in town Andrea didn't get to do those things. Maybe *she* should come over to Emily's house instead of the other way around.

When lunch was finished, they headed off to their own classes. But when it was time for last-period history class, Emily was happy when Mrs. Lorenz gave them the whole period to brainstorm ideas for their presentation.

"I'm not sure where to start," Emily admitted.

"Hold on." Andrea stood. "I will ask."

Andrea hurried up to Mrs. Lorenz's desk without a moment's hesitation, and Emily figured she was used to having to ask for help. She returned a minute later with a big book.

"This was given to me by Mrs. Lorenz for us to use. She says that any time before 1900 is good for our pre—" Andrea giggled. "Presentation."

Emily read the cover: *Adams County Memories*. She opened it and looked through it. It had been printed by the local historical society, and there was page after page of people's stories and black-and-white photos.

More students filled the room, talking and laughing. Then the bell rang, informing them class had officially started. A minute later Lily Cunningham strode into the room. She didn't look at Mrs. Lorenz, let alone offer an excuse for being tardy. With a bored look on her face, she pulled an empty desk up next to the two desks Andrea and Emily had put together and then sat.

"Hi, sister," Andrea chirped.

Emily noticed that the dispassionate mask Lily wore cracked.

"Hey, sis." Lily leaned forward in the desk. "So what are we doing again?"

"We're just looking for information for our presentation. Emily and I were looking through this book. You want to join us?"

Lily scooted closer. Then, sitting side by side, they flipped through the book. Emily had lifted one page to finish reading the story of a woman who'd come to Adams County as a mail-order bride when Andrea squealed. "Look, Bukvova! That is my friend's last name." Her finger moved down the page.

Andrea flipped to another page. "Look, more Czech families. Many of them." She turned one more page, and there was an advertisement poster. Andrea squealed again, causing many of the students who were working in their own small groups to look at her.

"This poster, you see, is written in Czech. It encourages families to homestead in Nebraska. It looks like they posted these in Czech newsletters."

"Do you mean newspapers?"

"Yes, newspapers."

Emily looked closer. "Wow, I didn't realize they advertised."

Lily pulled out her notebook. "What are we supposed to be talking about again?"

"How the railroad affected the growth of the settlements in Nebraska." Emily's finger moved down the page. "Perfect. Listen to this: 'What pulled Czechs to Nebraska was a steady stream of advertisements and glowing reports in Czech-language newspapers and magazines published here and sent back home. Railroads, like the Burlington & Missouri, advertised large tracts of Nebraska land for sale in Czech magazines like the *Hospodar* (husbandman or farmer), an Omaha agricultural journal, helping to promote settlement. Many families immigrated on the basis of information in such magazines, as well as letters from friends and relatives.'"

"Lily, do you want to jot this down as a note?" Emily asked.

Lily grabbed her backpack from under her desk and pulled out some sticky notes. She placed one on the top of the page. "I'll just go to the library and make a copy."

"Good idea!" Andrea held up her hand for a high-five.

One side of Lily's mouth lifted into a smile. "Thanks." They clapped their hands together.

The girls spent the rest of the class period looking through other books.

"I was thinking." Andrea placed a hand on Emily's shoulder. "We can go to the library on Friday. Then you can come and stay the night at our house. So you can come Friday instead of Saturday."

Emily glanced at Lily to see her reaction. Lily wrinkled up her nose and rolled her eyes. It was obvious that she wasn't too happy about Emily staying overnight.

Emily blew out a slow breath. "Or you can both come to my house."

"You don't want to come to *our* house?" Andrea pouted.

"I'll come if you'd like me to, but I'm sure Lily has other plans."

"Yes I do, actually." Lily twirled her pencil.

"Really?" Andrea furrowed her brow. "What?"

"I was thinking of watching a movie."

"We can watch it together after we work on our project."

Emily didn't know if Andrea was oblivious to Lily's coolness or if she was just trying to ignore it.

"Does that sound okay, Lily? We can do our project and then watch a movie?" Andrea repeated.

"Fine. Whatever." The bell rang, and Lily rose, walking out of the room with long strides.

"Great! Just bring your things to school on Friday. This is one of the things I have wished to do while I was in the United States . . . have a sleepover."

"You haven't had a sleepover before?"

Andrea shook her head. "No."

"Have you gone to one?" Emily brushed her hair from her face, trying not to act so surprised.

"Not yet. Sometimes Lily has a friend over but we . . . she . . ." Andrea bit her lip. "We have different, uh, friends."

Emily nodded, not knowing what else to say. She noticed Andrea didn't name any friends, and she wondered if she had any. *How sad it would be to go through the whole school year with Lily Cunningham as your only friend, and only because she was forced to like you.*

Emily honestly didn't want to go to Lily's house, but it was obvious how happy Andrea would be if she did.

"Uh, okay. I'll bring stuff to school on Friday—since it's okay with your mom and everything."

Andrea gave Emily a quick hug and then hurried out of the room.

Emily looked at the pile of books they still had on the desk. Sticky notes stuck out of most of them. She hurriedly put away the ones they didn't need and then carried the rest to Mrs. Lorenz's desk.

"May I take these books and get photocopies?" She glanced at her watch, hoping Sam wouldn't be too upset if they had to stay a little later.

"Sure. I'll be here for another forty-five minutes grading papers. Looks like you found some good stuff."

"Yeah, we did." Emily turned, deciding to leave her backpack in the room until she got back.

"Emily?" Mrs. Lorenz's voice paused her steps.

Emily turned. "Yeah?"

"I just wanted to let you know I appreciate your pairing up with Andrea." Mrs. Lorenz removed her glasses and set them on the desk. "She's had a challenging year. Her host mother confessed to me that she really hasn't made any close friends at the school, but I was hoping you'd be the one who could help her, you know, get to know people."

"Yeah, sure."

"Have you told her about your move to Nebraska from San Diego?"

"No, it really hasn't come up yet."

"You should. I think it could help."

Mrs. Lorenz put her glasses back on and then returned her focus to her work.

The books weighed on Emily's arms as she hurried to the library, but her heart felt lighter. It *did* feel good to befriend the foreign-exchange student. She was a nice girl. And for the first time Emily realized that maybe all her challenges over the last year and a half could help someone else too.

"Hey, Em." It was Sam's voice.

Emily paused. She hadn't see Sam and that girl Kendall until she had nearly passed them. They were sitting on the floor, tucked into a small alcove, their backs against the door of the art room.

"Oh, man. I totally forgot I needed to find you." The girl was looking up at Emily with curiosity, and Emily shuffled from side to side. "I need to make some photocopies. Is it going to be a problem to hang out for another thirty minutes or so?"

"No, no problem." Sam leaned closer to Kendall and refocused on the screen of the digital camera that she was holding up.

"Where did you take this?"

"Oh, at the car show in Harding last fall. Is that a sweet ride or what?"

"I'd love to have a car like that." Sam's voice was full of enthusiasm.

Emily turned, wondering if Kendall really liked cars, or if she just took photos of them to get the attention of guys.

Even though Emily didn't know Kendall that well, she had an uneasy feeling about her.

"Don't worry, Sam, I'll hurry," she called over her shoulder.

"No need. Just come get me when you're done."

Emily paused, turning to look at them again. They were still sitting too close for Emily's comfort, staring at the tiny screen of the camera. "Should I go find Christopher?"

"I already talked to him. He's going over to Dylan's house. Then he's getting a ride home."

"Uh, okay."

Emily hurried down the hall, but her mind was no longer on the books.

Who is this girl? And what has she done to my brother?

Chapter Seven

Bob was standing by the kitchen sink when Charlotte hurried inside.

"Hey there." A smile lit his face. "Whatcha got there?"

Charlotte held up the shoe box that Anita had given her. "Oh, remember that mystery concerning my granddaddy Elijah? Anita Wilson gave me some letters she thought could help me figure out what happened."

Bob's eyes widened, and he ran a hand down his face, brushing the gray stubble on his chin. "You're really set on getting to the bottom of this story, aren't you?"

"Well, it seems this has fallen in my lap, and now I feel like I have to at least try to find some answers," Charlotte admitted.

"Okay, Char. You do what you need to do," Bob said as he sauntered to his recliner and flipped on the television. "Let me know if you find anything interesting."

"I will," Charlotte mumbled. "I can tell you're so intrigued."

She reheated a cup of coffee in the microwave and sat down at the table with the box.

Gingerly, she opened the first letter and began to read.

104 Franklin Ave.
Boston
March 3, 1879

Dearest Wilma,

Our first day of spring! It was feeling as if winter was never to release its grasp, but dear me, how mild and warm the afternoon turned out to be.

Yesterday I had an entirely interesting afternoon in the library reading reports of the recent treatment of the Indians in the West. I still get shivers in my spine when I remember the words of your last letter: "Sometimes I believe I heard the sounds of Indian drums on the wind." Maybe it is indeed the drums or maybe it's simply your imagination of the olden days. Do you believe it is possible?

I think I told you there is a chance that I will get my own apartment here. It would be delightful to have a place of my own to call home. And no, please do not again try to encourage me to move your direction and claim a settlement. I know it's possible, it's just not proper. Do you wish me to remain an old maid forever? That would surely do it!

I do want to congratulate you on your new home—your church home, that is! I can't imagine how you've been meeting in a barn for the past year. I'm sure you can't wish for that train full of supplies to come soon enough. Friday is the day!

Your mother is expecting a letter these days. It probably is on the way. She is quite put out when she sees you've written me again and have written her nothing. Say hello to your neighbors for me. You soon will be completely Nebraskan.

Your loving Peggy

"Interesting." Charlotte turned to tell Bob about the woman's comments about the church, but he'd already fallen asleep in front of the TV. Charlotte moved to the next letter.

104 Franklin Ave.
Boston
April 1, 1879

Dearest Wilma,

I was saddened to get your last note and read the inscription on the exterior of the envelope that the train hadn't arrived after all. It will be there soon enough, sister.

I am looking day after day with "hope deferred" of news that you are ready for me to come to visit. I understand your desire for me to wait until the church is built, since everyone will be putting every extra minute into its completion. Please write again and tell me of the latest news. I feel as if I know every member of the community through your letters and feel their excitement over a church of their own.

So you haven't told me yet—is it confirmed you are in the family way? Please write back quickly and tell me. I wish nothing more than to welcome a new member into our family.

You must write our parents as often as you write me! You are my own dear sister, as you have always been, and I am your always devoted, faithful, affectionate sister.

Oh, I must finish and seal the envelope. The postman shall be here any minute.

Your loving Peggy

Charlotte spread the letter on the table and couldn't help but smile. The care of the sisters for each other was evident. Charlotte wondered why her kids had never cared for each other that way. She thought about Emily and Christopher too, wondering if they would write or at least e-mail Sam when he went away to college, *if* he went away to college.

She scanned the letter and thought back to the conversation her older family members used to have about Granddaddy. She tried to remember if they had ever talked about the train being late on the day the building supplies were to be delivered. She made a mental note of the fact and wondered if it had anything to do with the missing money. *Was Elijah there waiting with the money only to have the train never show up? What did he do with it afterward?*

Charlotte took a sip of her now-lukewarm coffee and turned her attention to the next letter in the stack.

104 Franklin Ave.
Boston
April 17, 1879

Dearest Wilma,
Please tell me it is not so! It is with tears in my eyes that I have read your letter for the third time. First, I am sorry to hear that a baby is not coming as you thought. Please care for yourself. I worry you work too hard on your land and in your home. Is it possible for Woodrow to hire extra help for you? Second, I cannot imagine your

heartache when the train pulled away from the station with all the supplies on board. If only the train had not been delayed that first day! If it had come at the correct time all of this trouble—and the rumors of thievery—could have been avoided.

What I do not understand is how a bag with mail and money could have disappeared in such a manner. And to answer your question, no I never received the letter that describes your visit with Mrs. Jackson—the one you say was in that missing mailbag.

To be fully honest I don't believe it ever will arrive. Surely if a thief has stolen the bag, as is suspected, he wouldn't keep the money and mail the letters, would he? That would be a very fine and considerate crook. I also don't understand why the money was in the mailbag. Is this common? It seems things work differently out west.

I have done now, I believe, the most important thing, which is to bring this matter in prayer before our Lord. I have prayed for those in your community. And, as you've requested, I've prayed for Elijah Coleman. I have to say that praying for him is harder than I expected for one reason: Sister, do you honestly believe he is as innocent as he says? If he was the last man seen with the bag, and it was in his care alone, how do we not know that he has hidden away the money for his own uses? You say he is a trustworthy man, and I would like to believe you. And why was Mr. Coleman in charge of these funds? It seems it would be the business of the preacher. I hope that my distrust is unfounded.

Tomorrow our dairy man is moving out west, and so we will have a new one. Mrs. Maudry passed away, and Rose Baxter is engaged to Ivan Smith. Can you believe it?

> *Yours sadly about all the troubles of the day,*
> *Peggy*

"Grandma, I'm home." It was Christopher's voice.

She glanced up and realized she'd been so engrossed in the letter that she hadn't even heard the door open. Cold wind blew in, ruffling the letters now spread out on the table. Toby rushed to Christopher, wagging her tail.

"Hey girl, you missed me, didn't you?" Christopher squatted down and gave Toby a quick hug.

"Hey there." Charlotte placed the letter on the table and realized her heart was pounding. The letters were exactly what she had been looking for—information about the events from that time period. This was much more reliable than her failed memory of conversations between uninformed family members who were now all gone.

"Where are Sam and Emily?" Charlotte asked, shuffling the letters into a safe pile.

"I don't know. I was over at Dylan's house, remember? His mom just dropped me off." Christopher took off his tennis shoes and put on his muck boots.

Charlotte glanced at the clock. It was time to start making dinner. She should start browning hamburger for sloppy joes. She tried to remember if either Sam or Emily had mentioned anything happening after school, but nothing came to mind.

Christopher moved his backpack next to the laundry room door and then changed out of his school coat, putting on his work jacket.

"Heading out to do chores?"

"Yup."

Charlotte considered calling Sam's cell phone to see where the kids were.

Just one more letter . . .

104 Franklin Ave.
Boston
April 30, 1879

Dearest Wilma,

Thank you for giving me an education on the workings of a small community like Bedford. It was interesting to note that the post office was the second building in "town" after the train depot. I did not know that the postmaster also serves as the local banker, since he is the only one who has a safe. Of course, in the matters your community is now facing, the safe did not provide much security. A saddening fact. I now also understand why the money was in the mailbag. You are correct, it only makes sense that he would use that means to carry the funds. Still, it is strange that no one saw it again after that day at the train. Where did he go after leaving the depot? What did he do? I'm sure he retraced his steps a thousand times.

Yesterday I was walking through the park . . .

Charlotte skimmed the rest of the letter. Peggy went on and on about some handsome guy in the park. Any other time she would have enjoyed reading about the man who had caught this young woman's attention, but all Charlotte could think about now was reading the rest of the letters and finding out more about Elijah Coleman.

Charlotte opened the next letter and was surprised to see that it was dated 1880 rather than 1879. She quickly read through some of the other letters, and it became clear why Anita hadn't put them on the top of the stack. They were very long—pages and pages of Peggy's story of her romance with a Mr. Gregory R. Strickle. Charlotte giggled as she skimmed through the lengthy descriptions of proper dinners, nights at the opera, and walks through the park. Only every so often was there a question about the church or a request of news about the trial.

"Oh, bother," Charlotte mumbled to herself. "It's a fine time to fall in love, Peggy. Talk about a distraction!"

Seeing that these letters were going nowhere except closer to Peggy's walking down the aisle, Charlotte turned back to the last letter Anita had put in the "important" stack.

104 Franklin Ave.
Boston
March 9, 1880

Dearest Wilma,
The wedding is in three weeks, and I am saddened you will not be here. Yet dear Gregory has promised that sometime next spring we will make a trip to your territory and cast our gazes on the land you love so much.

Gregory doesn't seem like the homesteader type, but perhaps there is a business opportunity in town that will catch his fancy.

But enough about that. Tears welled in my eyes as I read about the conviction of Mr. Elijah Coleman. I suppose you are right when you said that when there was no other proof of someone else taking the money they had no other choice.

My voice trembled as I read that part of the letter to Gregory. He has been following the saga too, and he listens as I read each post you send.

You can also imagine my utter joy when I read about how the men in the town gathered around their friend! I can picture the surprise on the sheriff's face when man after man lined up, asking to be locked up in order to help Mr. Coleman fulfill his sentence sooner, but my question is, why did the sheriff allow it? Perhaps he too had doubts about Elijah's guilt?

I'm sure those on the train and other visitors in town weren't amused when most of the stores—and even the depot—were shut down. They must have believed the men would have stayed longer had the ruling not been overturned! If men will come together and express such compassion I have no doubt the church WILL go up this summer as everyone hopes. May the Lord be gracious to provide you all that you need.

Yours,
Peggy

Charlotte hurriedly moved to the next letter.

104 Franklin Ave.
Boston
June 19, 1880

Dearest Sister,
Mother and Father told me to write and tell you that they will be sending you a letter all their own. They have news about all their neighbors, as they always do, but I didn't want to waste my words because I have news of my own!

Gregory and I decided we will be moving to Nebraska! We do not need to view the area before we decide. The character of those in your community was enough to convince us.

Father and Mother, of course, are put out. They do not know how they will go on with both of us so far away. I encouraged them to move with us, and that is a possibility. Just think, before long there will be no need for letters because we will see each other and take walks on the old buffalo trails that you love. But I will not waste time writing here because soon I will see you with my own eyes.

Blessings until we meet again soon. Gregory and I wish that you may keep your health and live contented.

Mrs. Gregory Strickle

Charlotte placed a hand over her heart pounding in her chest and suddenly felt as if her limbs were tied to a thousand balloons and she might lift from the chair any second. What Anita had said was true. The men in the town had stood up for their friend—had offered to serve part of his sentence for him. She folded up the letter and placed it in the envelope, wondering if Anita would allow her to make copies. Reading them had meant so much.

Bless those who mistreat you . . . . A scripture verse suddenly popped into her mind.

If anyone had been mistreated, it was those simple settlers who'd left home and family, who'd sacrificed all they had to tame the wild Nebraska land. All they desired was a place of their own to worship, yet they did not hold a grudge against the one accused of depriving them of that. They loved even someone who was charged with taking not only their money but also their dreams.

She wiped a tear from the corner of her eye and lifted her head as she heard the sound of Sam parking in the driveway. With one quick movement she put the letters away and then hummed her favorite worship tune as she grabbed the ground hamburger from the fridge. Thankfulness filled her heart—for her family, for her community, and for the fact that even if she hadn't discovered what happened to the money, she had learned that folks had gathered around her granddaddy, just as God told us we all should.

Chapter Eight

The filling for the sloppy joes was simmering on the stovetop, and the table was set with a large salad and homemade buns. Sam and Emily had joined Christopher in doing their chores, and Bob was still snoozing in his chair.

Seeing that she had time before dinner, Charlotte hurried to the desk. In the second drawer she found what she was looking for—a clean notebook. She grabbed a pen and sat down in the desk chair. On the inside cover of the notebook she wrote her name. She thought about writing "Clue Book" underneath it but then changed her mind.

"Who do you think you are, Nancy Drew?" she mumbled to herself.

She tapped her finger on her lips and then jotted down what she'd learned so far, including where she had found the information:

- As postmaster, Elijah also served as banker. (Peggy's letter)

- He was in charge of the funds for the church. (newspaper)

- The money was going to build Bedford Community Church. (newspaper)
- Elijah was set to meet the train and pay a man delivering the building supplies, and he put the money in the mailbag and took it to the train. (Peggy's letter)
- The train was late. (Peggy's letter)
- The money disappeared, and the mail did too. (Peggy's letter)
- Neither the money nor the mail was ever found. (Peggy's letter)

Charlotte paused. As she considered the fifth point, she thought about writing "was stolen" rather than "disappeared," but she didn't know that for a fact. Personally, she believed it was the truth, but all that was known was that the bag—and everything inside—up and vanished. None of the letters inside the bag were ever mailed or found. As far as she knew, the bag itself had never been found either.

What Charlotte didn't know was where Elijah had gone after he discovered the train wasn't coming that evening. It was obvious that he didn't go home and put the money in the safe.

She also echoed questions that Peggy had brought up. Where did he go? What did he do?

Oh, Lord, I know this is a silly thing, but it's beginning to matter a lot to me. You were there, Lord. You know who else was there. You know who has information, just like Anita had information. And if You point me in the right direction, I will be forever grateful.

"Amen," she mumbled, rising from the desk. Charlotte knew she needed to make cookies for the kids' lunches tomorrow, but she couldn't get her mind to focus on flour and eggs and chocolate chips.

Maybe she would do that after dinner.

She glanced out the window, wondering if the kids would be in soon so they could eat. Her stomach rumbled, and she realized she'd been so busy reading Anita's letters that she hadn't eaten since the scone at Anita's house.

"Nothing like a 130-year-old mystery to help me lose the ten pounds I gained from Christmas." Charlotte chuckled.

"Good, that will help you not feel so guilty about the chocolate I'm planning on getting you for Valentine's Day this Friday," Bob mumbled from his rocker. He opened his eyes and winked.

"You're prepared for Valentine's Day and I'm not?" Charlotte asked. "And, besides, I thought you were napping."

"How can I nap when I hear you banging around in there?" Bob pushed the lever, and his chair popped into the upright position. "Did you find any good clues, Sherlock?"

"Grandma! Grandma!" Christopher burst through the door. "I forgot to tell you the coolest thing about today. I just found out that my interview with those ice fishermen on Heather Creek is going to be the lead story in the school paper."

"Good for you. Perhaps soon you'll be having articles published in the *Bedford Leader*."

"Don't really understand ice fishing," Bob mumbled as he puttered around the kitchen looking for a pre-dinner snack.

"That gives me an idea." Charlotte moved to the mail pile to find last week's copy of the paper. It wasn't there, and she remembered she'd thrown it out yesterday.

"Bob, do you know when the *Bedford Leader* was first printed? I wonder if they printed any articles about Elijah Coleman. If it was around at the time, I'm sure they did. It was a big story. Do you think the *Bedford Leader* has archives on microfiche?"

"Hold on, Charlotte. You're talking too fast. What did you say?"

"You know, Bob. Microfiche. Didn't the library put a lot of their old materials on it? I wonder if the newspaper did the same thing."

"Fish at the *Bedford Leader*?" Christopher shrugged. "Wait, I think there is, Grandma. I know Mr. Barnes has a blue beta on his desk, but I haven't seen any other kind of fish around there."

A burst of laughter escaped from Charlotte's lips. Bob's deep chuckle joined in.

"No, not fish that swim in water, Christopher. Microfiche. It's what newspapers and libraries used to copy all their own newspapers and other materials onto. They used it before computers. It was like copying large documents onto film. At least I think it was something like that. I remember looking up documents with Bill when he was your age."

Christopher scratched his head. "I can ask. What kind of fish are they again?"

"Why don't you call Mr. Barnes tomorrow, Charlotte? I'm sure he'd love to help. He might even want to write about this story—when you get something figured out, that is."

"Write about it?" Charlotte remembered the reaction of her friends at church—the way they had treated her differently, as if *she'd* stolen the money. *We'll just worry about that when the time comes.*

Bob cleared his throat. "Are we going to eat soon? I think I'm going to get blown away by a strong west wind if I don't fill my gut soon." Bob patted his large stomach.

"Yes, I know, dear. You've had a strenuous afternoon napping. How do you manage?"

"It is good to see you doing something fun for yourself, but I sure hope I don't have to start cooking again."

Charlotte didn't know if she appreciated or disliked his words. The way Bob had said them made her feel like this was just a game, or something to entertain her in the midst of all the work.

"It's partly for me, but mostly for all of us," she interjected. "After all, Elijah Coleman's genes are in our kids and grandkids. His story is part of our stories, whether we like it or not."

"I suppose you're right," Bob agreed. "Funny thing, how quickly everything changes though." He smirked. "Doesn't seem very long ago that when I needed information about something, I'd look to an old-timer for help. These days, I'm the old-timer!"

"Yes, cool!" Christopher punched a fist in the air. "That's perfect."

"What's perfect? That your grandfather is finally admitting he's an old-timer?"

"No. Not that." His eyes widened. "What if, when we talk to Mr. Barnes, I ask if I can write a story about this for the paper?"

"Wow, Christopher. I didn't know you were that interested." Charlotte pointed to her notebook. "After dinner I can share what I've found out so far, if you'd like."

Christopher shook his head. "I am interested, but that's not the best part. Last time I saw Mr. Barnes, he told me he'd been following my work in the school paper. He says I have talent."

"He's right." Bob hooked his thumbs through his suspenders.

"Yeah, well, I asked him if I could write for the *Bedford Leader*. You know, maybe write an article once a month for him?"

"And what did Mr. Barnes say?" Charlotte could see that Sam and Emily were heading across the yard toward the house. She moved to the stove to stir the meat filling one last time. She also stirred the small pot in which she'd used a veggie burger to make some meatless filling. It sure didn't smell as appetizing, but if that's what Emily enjoyed then good for her.

"Mr. Barnes said that it wasn't a bad idea, but I needed to wait for the right story. I asked him what type of story, and he said I would know when I found it."

"Do you think this is it?" Charlotte felt both pleased with Christopher's interest and horrified by the fact that this story would be spread all over town. Would everyone tell her she was on a wild goose chase? Would they laugh at her for trying to dig up a past that was long buried? An ache filled her stomach, and she knew it had nothing to do with being hungry.

Charlotte pursed her lips. "I don't know if that's a good idea."

"What do you mean, you don't know?" Bob nudged her with his elbow. "You're usually the first one encourage the kids to try things."

"Yes, but shouldn't we wait until we have the mystery figured out?"

"Char, are you trying to say that we should wait until we can determine, with certainty, that Elijah Coleman was indeed innocent?"

"Well, if you're going to put it that way, I do think it's a good idea. I mean, that's one of the reasons I wanted to solve this mystery in the first place. I don't like the mud that's been slapped on our family name. If we publicize this and it turns out he's guilty, it'll just make things worse."

It'll ruin our reputation just like it ruined his, she wanted to say but didn't.

"But, Grandma, most of the fun is figuring out the mystery. If you already know the answer, it's not the same anymore."

Charlotte tucked her hair behind her ear. "I suppose you're right, but what if we *never* solve it? I'm not a professional sleuth, you know."

"Just keep doing what you're doing." Bob squeezed her shoulder. "You're doing a fine job."

"Yeah, and leave all the writing to me!" Christopher grinned. "Maybe Mr. Barnes will like something I come up with."

"I suppose we can stop by the newspaper office after school. I'll call and make an appointment with Mr. Barnes, and we'll head over together after I pick you up."

Christopher bounced on the floor as if he were riding a pogo stick. He still had his muck boots on, and bits of mud and hay scattered all over the floor as he jumped. "Yes, yes, yes!"

The door opened and Emily and Sam entered. Their noses and cheeks were bright red from the cold.

"Emily, Sam, guess what? I'm going to write a mystery on our history. Hey, I like that. A history mystery!"

Chapter Nine

"Be with you in a minute, folks." Finding the file he needed, Rick Barnes slipped it out and then turned and smiled. "Charlotte, Christopher, nice to see you." He motioned for them to join him behind the counter.

Charlotte spotted the framed copy of the first *Bedford Leader* that hung on the wall. When she saw the date, 1880, she felt just a bit disappointed. The night before she'd hardly been able to sleep, thinking that the first newspaper had been published before that and that there had been continuing coverage of the case.

Christopher followed Rick behind the counter.

"How's my little newspaperman?" Rick commented.

"Okay, I suppose, but I'm trying to solve a history mystery, actually," Charlotte heard Christopher say.

Instead of following the guys to the back, she paused and scanned the paper. As she read, she moved her finger along the columns just above the glass so she wouldn't smear it.

"When did you say this incident happened?" she heard Rick ask Christopher.

"April 1879," Christopher commented. After dinner last night he'd drilled Charlotte about everything she knew so he could appear knowledgeable in front of Mr. Barnes.

"Oh, I seem to remember something about that. But I've heard a lot about Bedford. It's hard to remember exactly."

Charlotte heard the wheels of Mr. Barnes's desk chair pushing back, and she turned and watched him rise. He hurried to the front entry of the newspaper offices, where Charlotte was still reading the front pages of the first copy of the *Leader*.

"I found something," she muttered, pointing to the top right-hand column.

Christopher stretched to look. Then he began reading the page out loud:

"Tuesday, January 20, 1880, by J. T. Bayne.

Town news.

Rev. P. Macmillan, of Omaha, was in town yesterday.

The days have lengthened about 20 minutes since Dec. 21, '79.

Reynolds' sugar-cured hams and breakfast bacon, just received and for sale at Windauers General Store on Lincoln Street.

A number of farmers from several miles distance were caught in town by the rain yesterday and were obliged to plod their way home through deepening mud.

The work of leveling the gravel streets with the big scraper was commenced early Monday morning. The operation was greatly to the advantage of all having occasion to pass over the street on wheels.

Services for Bedford Community Church will be held at 10 o'clock this forenoon at Abe Johnson's barn, to which all are invited."

Christopher paused, and the muscles in Charlotte's stomach tightened.

"The church met in a barn?" Rick Barnes scratched his head. "I've skimmed this paper a few dozen times, but I suppose I never noticed that before."

"They would have been in the church instead of the barn if . . ." Christopher looked toward Charlotte.

"If the church's money that Granddaddy had been in charge of hadn't disappeared into thin air."

"Seriously? This is a story I need to hear."

"How 'bout a story you need to read?" Christopher removed his backpack and pulled out a blue notebook, ripping out the first page. He handed the page to Rick. "I wrote out the idea for the story last night. My grandma read it over and made sure I got the facts right."

Rick Barnes leaned back against the front counter and read. "Interesting. Very interesting. But if you don't mind, I'd like you to do a little more work. Instead of a straight news piece, could you possibly write it in the first person, from your point of view? How does it feel to you to know one of your ancestors did something—whether intentional or not—that changed the history of Bedford forever?"

Christopher rubbed his chin. "I suppose I never thought of it that way before."

"Well, think about it. Think about what this means to *you*, here, today," Rick suggested. "Also be sure to tie in the anniversary of Bedford Community Church. It will have a better chance of making it in if it has a connection that's timely."

"We can talk about that later, Christopher." Charlotte forced a smile. Even though she wasn't completely comfortable about making the story public yet, she thought maybe she could have a conversation with Christopher about the most important parts. Especially about the local men "sitting" in to help serve Elijah's jail sentence. It could be a positive ending to a sad story.

"Okay, Mr. Barnes. I'll work on this. And *then* will you run my story?"

"If it's good enough, I might sometime. News space is precious, my boy. It's not something I promise away. People need to earn it."

Charlotte cleared her throat, attempting to turn the conversation back to the real reason she'd come: to see if the *Bedford Leader* had archives she could take a peek at.

"We know the money disappeared. We also know that my granddaddy was convicted of the theft. But we'd like to figure out what was happening the week of the disappearance. You know, were there visitors in town? Or maybe robberies in other parts of the county?"

"I wish I could help you, but I can't. You see, by 1880 the town had grown to about a thousand people and was doing well. The business district was going gangbusters, but it all ended on June 24, 1880, when a disastrous fire destroyed most of the buildings on the east side of Lincoln Street. It nearly wiped out most of this small town's commerce." Rick pointed up the street. "They figure it was arson because those trying to put out the fire soon discovered two other sections of town engulfed in flames."

"Did they ever catch the person who did it?" Christopher tapped his temple as if he were deep in thought.

"Not that I know of."

Charlotte's heart ached for the community she'd grown to care about. She could almost imagine Peggy's letters. Then again, perhaps Peggy was living here by that time.

"The worst part was that the first two years of the newspaper's archives were completely destroyed." He pointed to the wall. "That copy was saved because the editor at the time had taken it home as a memento."

"Obviously they rebuilt the town," Charlotte commented.

"Yes. The rebuilding began as soon as the old sites were cleared. And this time they were made out of brick." He patted the wall.

"Whoa, this place is old." Christopher's eyes widened as he took in the tall ceiling and windows.

Charlotte glanced around the room, trying to picture what it used to look like. "Makes you think of all the businesses that used to be run in these places . . . all the people, their comings and goings."

Rick nodded. "As that saying goes, if walls could talk."

"I wish they could." Charlotte put her notebook back into her oversized purse. "Goodness knows it would be much easier than tracking down bits and pieces scattered all over the place."

"It would help my story too," Christopher mumbled.

"But the investigation is half the fun." Rick chuckled

and placed a hand on Christopher's shoulder. "Especially when you have a sidekick."

"I suppose that's so. I've enjoyed unraveling the story so far. I only hope there's a satisfactory answer at the end." Charlotte couldn't shake off the discouragement trailing her like a stray dog. Still, she forced a smile on her face for Christopher's sake. Then they said good-bye to Mr. Barnes and headed out.

"That's great news about the article. It was nice for Mr. Barnes to point you in the right direction," she said as she unlocked the car.

"I know, but it sounds hard."

"Everything worth doing is worth doing well," Charlotte said, realizing she was repeating something her mother used to tell her.

They got in, and Charlotte started the car. As she drove home, Christopher was already busy jotting down ideas for what he was going to write. She didn't mind his silence. In fact, it suited her pensive mood.

Charlotte's mind scurried to figure out where to go for answers, but in every direction she seemed to hit dead ends.

Chapter Ten

On Friday, Charlotte couldn't wait to get back to the boxes at the church. She possessed a slim hope that somewhere within all that junk more clues were waiting to be unearthed. She headed out after she had done her morning chores and left some lunch for Bob. In her car was the sleeping bag Charlotte had promised to drop by the school for Emily for her sleepover at the Cunninghams' house.

Last fall Charlotte had heard about Andrea, the school's one and only exchange student, but she hadn't yet met the girl. She was pleased that Emily was working with her and with Lily on their presentation. It was time Emily's spats with Lily be put behind them.

Still, Charlotte had to admit Emily was braver than she was. Charlotte found it hard to forget all the comments Allison Cunningham had made about her parenting. When Charlotte had noticed the look in Emily's eyes last night as she packed, she knew she didn't have to remind Emily to be on her best behavior.

Christopher was planning to stay at Dylan's house so that meant it would only be Sam home tonight, which seemed strange. Charlotte didn't know if she knew how to cook for only three anymore, or four if Pete wasn't meeting up with Dana to go over more wedding plans.

In the foyer of the church, Charlotte took off her gloves and stuffed them in her pockets. Then she hung up her coat on a coat hanger. Bedford Community Church was the church she and Bob had attended all their married years. They'd raised their three children in those pews, and now their grandchildren. Charlotte glanced around, taking in the large map with pins showing the locations of the various missions the church members supported. She also saw that the dark brown carpet had seen better days. Even the beige paint on the walls needed an extra coat. But that wasn't something they needed to worry about now. *One project at a time. One is enough.*

She hurried to the basement and was pleased to see Maxie already sitting at a table poking through a box. Charlotte sat down next to her and peeked at the photo in her hand, eager to see what held the woman's interest.

Maxie had an old photo of a church picnic on the edge of Heather Creek.

"Do you know what this reminds me of?" Maxie closed her eyes, as if reliving a memory that still played in her mind.

"What?" Charlotte asked.

"Watering stock." She opened her eyes and winked at Charlotte.

Charlotte waited, knowing a story was coming.

"You see, when we first had our farm we had only a few cows and one old horse, so we carried buckets of water from Heather Creek to our farm. We had an old trough that my father made. I can't believe it, but when I was a teen we chopped up that old trough for firewood because it had split into two pieces." Maxie slapped her leg. "One more genuine antique—gone!" She chuckled, and the lines around her eyes deepened.

Charlotte laughed more at Dana's grandmother than at her story.

"Anyway, I was thinking about how we dug a well, but it still didn't furnish enough water for the livestock. That meant we had to take the stock, including the oxen, to the buffalo hole near the creek."

"Buffalo hole?" Charlotte asked.

"It was just a low spot on our property where water pooled. We called it that because the old homesteaders said that's where the buffalo used to drink—Indians too, I guess. When I was a kid the teepee rings were still there. They were rock circles. The Indians used the rocks to hold down the teepees, you know."

Charlotte nodded, remembering she'd heard that before.

"I wonder if the rock circles are still around," Nancy Evans called from across the room. Charlotte didn't know she'd been listening.

"Nah." Maxie shook her head. "All the kids messed them up, looking for arrowheads." Her eyes sparkled. "Found a few too. Those were some fun times we had, even though we didn't have much."

"Sounds like you made the most of things," Charlotte agreed.

For the next thirty minutes Maxie told more stories—about Bedford Community Church in the 1930s and during

World War II. Charlotte hoped she would remember all of Maxie's great details. She also thought about talking to Pete and Dana, maybe asking them to consider videotaping Maxie. Dana's grandma seemed to be in good health, but one never knew. And what Maxie said was true—somehow the stories of the past needed to be passed on.

They sat in comfortable silence for a while as they looked through a box of obituaries for local boys who had died in World War II. Some were Sam's age. Others were only a few years older.

"Can you believe Pete's wedding is only a month away?" Hannah asked as she poured herself a cup of coffee and joined Charlotte and Maxie.

"I know. I feel a little guilty being here, but when I talked to Dana a few days ago it sounded like she had everything under control." Charlotte took a sip of coffee and realized that Hannah must have brought her own beans. It didn't have that thick, sludgy taste that the church coffee usually had.

"Oh, speaking of weddings. I brought you something to see." Maxie took a large manila envelope off the table and slid out a photo of a young couple.

"Oh, is this your wedding picture?" Charlotte gazed at the gazebo and the lovely couple. Maxie was a tiny slip of a thing, and Charlotte could tell the wedding dress was borrowed from the way it hung on her, a few sizes too large. Her veil was worn like a cap on her head, and the tulle of the veil spilled over her shoulders and all the way down her back to the floor. Small pin curls framed her face, and Maxie's husband, Wilbert, stood next to her.

"My, my, your husband is dashing." Charlotte cooed.

"He sort of looks like the professor from *Gilligan's Island*—taller and stockier, but just as handsome," Hannah chimed in.

"Oh, Hannah, you think everyone looks like someone from *Gilligan's Island*," Charlotte ribbed her friend. Turning to Maxie, she saw the saddened look in her older friend's eye. "Your anniversary was Valentine's day. It would have been seventy years today." Charlotte touched Maxie's arm.

"Seventy years," Hannah added. "Is that possible?"

"It is. I married when I was eighteen, and I'm eighty-eight. But let's not get sidetracked. Here's another photo, of our reception. You know it wasn't common back then to have a photo of those who *attended* the wedding, but my husband was a people person. He insisted a photo be taken of all our friends and family." Maxie placed the photo in front of Charlotte as Hannah hustled around the table to peek over her shoulder for a better look.

"There's Wilma Wilson, Anita's grandmother, and her sister, Peggy." Charlotte felt excitement growing as she looked at the photos, as if she'd just been reconnected with two dear friends. "Or is that Peggy and the other one Wilma? I think as they grew older it became even harder to tell them apart."

Charlotte stared at them closer, noticing the happiness on their faces. Obviously Nebraska had been good for both of them.

"And where is Peggy's husband? Is he in the picture?" Hannah asked.

"No." Maxie shook her head. "I'm sorry to say he died just a few years after their marriage. He was working at the depot here in Bedford, and there was an accident with one of the trains."

A deep sadness filled Charlotte as if she'd just lost a close friend. She placed a hand to her neck. "You aren't serious, are you? How did Peggy handle that?"

"It wasn't easy."

"Did Peggy remarry?" Charlotte asked.

"Yes, after many years she married a man from Harding and moved up there. Before that she tried to get by on her own. Others tried to help, but Peggy, like others before her, soon realized the best thing to do was find a new husband. Like many women of that time, Peggy married out of necessity. Love came later, and from what I hear, she had three sons."

Charlotte imagined it all—the joy of marriage, the heartbreak, remarrying out of necessity. *Times were hard* . . .

Maxie pointed to an older couple near the edge of the photo. "Look, Charlotte, it's your great-grandparents."

Charlotte lifted the photo to her face to get a better look. At home she had photos of her great-grandparents when they were younger . . . their engagement photo, and one taken when her grandfather Albert was a baby. But she'd never seen them with gray hair and wrinkles.

"I'm amazed how much my dad looked like his grandfather. I can see the family resemblance." Charlotte tilted her head as she stared into his face. "I wish I could have had a chance to know them."

"You're right—they did look alike. Everyone around town knew who was a Coleman. It was the nose, I think. Very Roman and handsome."

Charlotte looked at the photo again. Her great-grandparents stood on the fringes of the group, but at least they were there. It wasn't as if they'd been completely shunned forever.

"They look happy. Or at least content. I can see the slightest of smiles on their lips." Hannah patted Charlotte's shoulder.

"Yes, they went on to have a good life, I think." Maxie leaned back in her chair. "I know that the lost money troubled them for many years, but it didn't mark their entire lives. I credit the community for that. Even though there were some people who always thought Elijah Coleman stole the money, many others believed in him, and I had a special reason why I believed in him too."

"What's that?" Charlotte asked.

"I don't believe there was a dog in all Nebraska that would not wag his tail when he saw your granddaddy coming. Dogs know good people when they see them. When I saw my dog, Lucky, wag her tail and spin in circles at the sight of your granddaddy I knew he was a good person."

"Well, I suppose that's a good sign."

"From what I hear, many of the folks in town stood up for him, believed in him," Maxie repeated.

"Yes, I know. Anita showed me the letters."

"Letters?" Maxie asked.

"You don't know?" For the next ten minutes Charlotte told the ladies who'd gathered around about Peggy's letters to her sister Wilma.

"That's strange." Maxie patted her salt-and-pepper hair. "It's a nice story. I like to hear that they did that—"

"Charlotte, come here. I think I found something!" Nancy Evans's voice interrupted their conversation.

Charlotte hurried over to Nancy, who was sifting through a large box.

"It's a collection of old Bibles." Nancy was holding one and gently brushing it with her other hand. As Charlotte approached, she blew the dust from the cover.

"Like a Bible lost and found?" Hannah peeked in.

"Yes, and look. There's a name written in the inside cover. And a date."

Charlotte opened it. "Oh . . . it's . . ." The words caught in her throat. "It's my great-grandmother's. It says, 'Lavina Coleman, 1890.'"

"Ten years after the scandal," Hannah whispered.

"The scandal?" Melody approached with a plate of fresh-baked oatmeal-raisin cookies. The scent of cinnamon swirled around the woman, more enticing than the finest French perfume.

"I can't believe you haven't heard of Charlotte's granddaddy's scandal. There's been more buzz about it than who shot J.R. in the eighties," Hannah said. "You must have left before the news clipping was found on Tuesday."

"I must have; fill me in."

Charlotte went on to explain yet again. And as she finally finished retelling the whole story, she changed her mind about questioning whether Christopher's article should indeed be in the *Bedford Leader*. At least if it was there—in one place—she wouldn't have to tell the story so many times.

She stayed for a little while longer, until the desire to sneak away with her great-grandmother's Bible became too much.

She ran her fingers along the spine and felt her throat growing tight and thick.

"Oh, Charlotte, I found something else." Nancy handed her another book. "It looks like a journal of sorts, and it also has Lavina's name in it."

"Your great-grandma sounds like me, always forgetting stuff everywhere I go." Hannah slapped her leg. "I'd bet anyone twenty bucks there's at least *two* Bibles with my name on them in that box."

"You're on," Melody said as they hurried over to the box.

Charlotte remained where she was. She looked inside the front cover, and her heart pounded. *1881. Just a few years after the incident.*

What a gift, Lord. Thank You! Charlotte flipped through the pages. On some of them were sermon notes. Scripture verses and the preacher's main speaking points were written in neat script. Charlotte flipped through more pages and noticed that they looked more like a diary or journal. Then a few pages later it was more sermon notes.

She kept flipping through and saw that nearly every page was filled except for the last twenty pages.

Charlotte pressed it to her chest, not caring that the century-old dust was getting her dirty. Then, with quivering fingers, she turned to the first journal page.

"Dear Lord, another day dawns, and I question whether it will be a good one or hard one," she read.

Tears lined Charlotte's eyelids, blurring the words on the page. How many times had she thought the same thing?

"Lavina Coleman must have been very forgetful to leave

so many things lying around," Maxie repeated, brushing the dust from her hands.

"Either that or God helped her to forget," Charlotte muttered. "He knew I would need this. Not only for the answers, but also for my heart."

Maxie rose and moved toward the coatrack. "I'll be heading home now. I think you'd best do the same." Maxie winked. "It's not like you'll get much done anyway with your mind on those journal pages. Why don't you head home and relax and read? There's a reason you found it, you know."

"Yes," Charlotte said, following Maxie to the coatrack. "I have the same feeling too."

Chapter Eleven

"In the Czech Republic the word for 'tea' is *chai*, just like chai means tea here too," Andrea explained as they stared at the menu at Mel's Place. "Except our chai isn't the spicy stuff like you have. It's just black tea. Still, I like it, your chai."

"Ashley drinks chai sometimes. Now I know what that is." Emily chuckled. "And, yeah, I totally know one Czech word now!"

"Yes, and maybe by the end of the night I can teach you two." Andrea's smile was wide.

"I will have green chai please," Andrea told Ginny, who was waiting on them from behind the counter. "Emily, would you like chai too?"

"Sure. I'll try it." Emily pulled out her money from her pocket, but Andrea had already handed Ginny some.

"Don't worry about it. It's on me. Did I say that right? *It's on me?*"

"You did. Is that a phrase you learned while you were here?" Emily crossed her arms over her chest, still slightly chilled from their walk. They'd walked from the high school to the bank where Andrea's host dad worked.

They'd dropped off Emily's overnight paraphernalia in his office and then decided to stop by Mel's to get something hot to drink before they headed to the library. Lily had cheerleading practice and hadn't been able to join them.

"Yes, learning idioms is one of my favorite things. You know 'beat around the bush' and 'bear hug' and 'all in a day's work.' Those were not things I learned in my English language class."

"Here you go. Two green chai teas."

Andrea took both cups and handed one to Emily. "Here you go."

"Thanks." Emily took a sip and felt her eyes widening in surprise. "It's actually good. I didn't expect that."

"No sweat." Andrea giggled.

"Why don't we sit here and warm up before we head to the library?" Emily shivered. "I'm not ready to go out in the cold yet."

"Good idea."

They headed to the nearest booth and sat across from each other, face to face.

"It sure is cold here," Andrea said, zipping down her coat. "We have cold winters where I live, but nothing like this."

"You're telling me. Once I sneezed, and the little bits of spit that spurted from my lips turned into snow before they hit the ground."

"Really?" Andrea's eyes grew wide.

Laughter burst from Emily's lips. "No, that was a joke."

"Oh." Andrea laughed along. "I thought you were serious."

"I'm not serious, but it seems like it could happen. I can't wait for spring to come."

Andrea took a sip from her chai. "It seems like you'd be used to it, growing up here and all."

"I didn't grow up here."

"You didn't?"

"I moved here a couple of years ago when my mom . . ." Emotion caught in her throat. "My mom was in a car accident. My dad was gone, and my brothers and I moved here to live with my grandparents."

"I'm sorry about your mom."

Emily saw sympathy in Andrea's eyes.

"I cannot imagine. It is hard being away from my mom and I know I will see her again in a few months."

"Thanks. It is hard." Emily took a sip of her chai, not knowing what to say. She thought about doing what Mrs. Lorenz had said and sharing some of her own experiences with moving to Nebraska, but now that she was actually trying, it wasn't as easy as she had thought it would be. Most of the time it was easier to forget about her mom than to think about life—the whole rest of her life—without her.

"So where did you live before?" Andrea's voice was gentle.

"In San Diego, which is in Southern California."

Andrea's face brightened. "I'd love to go there someday."

"Why didn't you go there, you know, when you applied for the exchange?"

"I really didn't have a choice. I filled out an application and then I waited to see which family chose me. I knew some people who didn't get picked, so I was lucky."

Emily nodded, even though she wouldn't call sharing a room with Lily *lucky*.

"Were you disappointed that you got Nebraska?"

Andrea bit her lip. "Well, maybe a little. Most of the movies are about New York or Hollywood. Nebraska is just a little different."

"You think?" Emily cocked an eyebrow. "But my grandma says all things happen for a reason. So maybe, down the road or something, we'll discover why we both ended up here."

"Maybe it was just to drink chai, talk, and get an A on our pres—our project. It doesn't matter though. I don't mind being here very much now. Especially now that I have a friend."

"It's hard, isn't it?" Emily said. "I remember what that was like. It's hard being the new person when everyone else knows each other. They have their happy little circles..."

"It was harder than I thought. I mean, I have lots of friends back home. It was not something I believed would happen." Tears welled up in Andrea's eyes. "I'm glad we're working on this project together." She smiled.

Emily rose. "Speaking of the project, we should get going. We better get what we need before Mr. Cunningham—I mean your dad—picks us up at the library."

Ten minutes later they were in front of the library. Emily drank the last of her lukewarm chai before hurrying inside. Andrea paused as she looked around the large, open room. Then she turned to Emily.

"Do you know where the books on the railroads are? And settler stuff? That way?" She pointed to the non-fiction section.

"Yes, but it's easier if we look up what we want in the

card catalog first. It takes less time." Emily looked at her watch. "Uh-oh. It's almost time for your dad to get off work."

"Did I hear you two talking about settlers?" A woman approached Emily. She had blondish red hair and eyelashes so light that Emily had to look close to make sure they were there.

"Yeah. We have to do a presentation for school," Emily said, trying to remember if she'd seen this woman before. She didn't think so.

"It's sue next week."

"Sue?" the woman asked.

"She means *due*." Emily playfully punched Andrea's arm. "She's not from around here."

"I'm from the other side of the big pond," Andrea quipped.

"I'm not from around here either—close, but not exactly. But my aunt is from Bedford. Her name is Mary Louise Henner."

"Oh yes. She's a friend of my grandma," Emily said. "She plays the organ at our church."

"Do you like the organ?" the woman asked, tilting her head to the side.

Emily bit her lower lip. "I think it takes talent to play, but . . ."

Laughter burst from the woman's lips. "I know. I'm not a huge fan either. My aunt tried to teach me. Let's just say I was an awful student on purpose!" The woman stretched out her hand. "I'm June, by the way, like the month."

Emily and Andrea shook her hand.

"You're in luck." She motioned for them to follow her behind the counter. "I think I might be able to help you."

Emily followed cautiously, looking for Edna, the regular librarian. Anybody who lived in Bedford for a while knew Edna had two rules. First, everyone must have a card. And second, no one was allowed behind the counter.

"Are you sure?" Emily glanced around.

"Yes, I'm sure. Edna's off today, but she gave me permission to bring people back. Under my supervision, of course."

June opened the door to the room closest to the front of the library. A tall window let light into the room; long tables ran down both sides.

"Most of my family grew up here, but I'm from Harding," June explained. "But when they were looking for someone to work on their museum archives and also a part-time librarian, my aunt figured I'd be interested. I love this old stuff."

Andrea bent over the nearest table to look more closely at the photographs lying on its top. "Wow, these are old pictures."

Emily scooted closer too. "May I touch them?"

"Sure, they won't crumble in your hands. Just make sure you hold them by the edges."

Emily spotted one that sort of looked like the building that Mel's Place was in. She gingerly picked it up. "Wow, this is Bedford?" Her eyes took in the wide dirt streets, the buildings, the wagons, and people wearing old-fashioned clothes.

"Yeah, Mel's Place was a saloon years ago. I've been meaning to get down there and show the owner this photo."

June handed Emily another photo. "Here's a photo of the train depot. Do you know that old building at the north end of Lincoln Park? That's where the depot used to be. They discontinued service long ago. After World War II, I think. As you can see, it used to be the only thing in that area. If you'd like, I can make a photocopy of this. It might help your report. After all, Bedford wouldn't even be here if it weren't for the railroad. The depot was the first thing in town. The post office was the second."

Andrea moved down the tables, looking at the photos. "I like these. Where I live it didn't really look like this."

"Yeah," Emily commented. "I bet where you live there are old castles and stuff."

"Oh, I love castles." June sighed. "Now *that* would be my dream job."

Andrea paused before one photo. She picked it up and turned to Emily. "Look at this one. It is so sweet. It is like a party with food."

Emily looked over her shoulder. "Oh, it's a picnic. Wow, that's cool. Look at their big dresses and parasols."

June moved to Andrea's other side. "Yes, I remember this. I found it in an old storage shed. The owner was going to throw everything out, and I rescued the whole box. It's a photo of the Fourth of July, 1878 or 1879, I suppose. See? If you look behind that tree you can see the beginnings of Bedford Community Church."

"Wow, that's strange. My grandma was just talking about the old church. I heard her saying something to my grandpa about her granddaddy, but I wasn't paying attention."

"Oh yes, my aunt told me about their project. All the ladies are cleaning out the basement and making their own display, which makes me happy. My aunt's supposedly saving some stuff for me—stuff she's just sure I'll be able to use in my 'museum in miniature,' as I like to call it."

They looked at photos for a few more minutes, and June found others she thought would be useful.

"Oh yes, we would love all of these for our project." Andrea clapped her hands together.

Just as they were about to leave, Emily spotted another photograph. It was framed and leaning against the wall. She bent down and looked closer. It was a woman holding a little boy on her hip. Their smiles were wide. The woman was beautiful.

"Oh, I love this photo." Emily sighed.

"Me too. It really captures the spirit of the day."

"What's this platform behind her?" Emily asked. "Is it a stage or something?"

"Oh, no." June shook her head. "It's actually the foundation of Bedford Community Church. For some reason they built the foundation and then stopped there. I think it sat a year before they finished."

"Oh no," Andrea glanced at her watch. "We need to hurry. My father should be waiting outside." Andrea waved to June. "Thank you very much. We will be back for those copies." She hurried out the door.

"Yes, thank you, and if it's okay I'd love to bring my grandma back sometime," Emily said. "I think she'd really love it."

"Of course! Just let me know, and I'll make sure I'm on the schedule when she comes," June said. "Any lover of history is a friend of mine."

Chapter Twelve

Charlotte noticed Dana's car parked at the house, and she tucked the journal and Bible under her arm as she hurried inside.

"Hey, Mom," Pete called as she entered.

Charlotte sniffed the air. "Mmm, something smells good. It's not often there's the aroma of baking when I'm not the one in the kitchen."

Dana looked up from where she sat at the dining room table, and Charlotte noticed flour on her cheek. "They're lemon cookies baking in the oven. My mom found the recipe, and I've been wanting to whip some up. I might bake some for the reception. I hope you don't mind me using your kitchen."

Charlotte noticed the large mixing bowl in the sink and the mess of flour and egg shells on the counter. She forced a grin. "No, I don't mind at all. I can't wait to try some."

She set the Bible and the journal near the phone and the mail pile and then hung up her coat and considered asking Dana if she honestly thought she'd have time to bake cookies before the wedding. It seemed like no matter how long one planned, there were always a hundred last-minute things to be done near the big day. Yet Charlotte kept her mouth shut as she got a glass of water from the sink and thought about the advice her own mother-in-law had given her when Anna and Bill got married: *The bride always knows best and has the final say. It makes for a happy wedding. The mother of the groom provides moral support, and whatever else she is asked to do—nothing more.*

Ma Stevenson had then tacked on the following: *And it's even more important after the wedding to keep your thoughts to yourself. It makes for a happy wife for your son and a happy life.*

Charlotte had reminded herself of those words more than once during Pete's and Dana's planning.

She took her water and settled in across from the couple. Spread before them were a dozen books of poetry. Pete's eyes were glazed over. Charlotte stifled a giggle.

"What are you doing?" she asked, even though the answer was obvious.

"We're trying to find a special poem for our wedding program," Dana answered.

Pete's mouth widened into a full-tooth grin. "We've found a lot of nice ones, but none have been quite *special* enough."

Dana elbowed his ribs, and Pete winced. "Ow, that hurt."

"Yeah, what you said hurt too. We're doing this for *our* wedding, remember? Just any ordinary poem isn't going to do."

"I know. Why don't we read our three favorites to Mom, and she can give us her opinion."

Dana pushed back the pile of books and readjusted the red band that held her hair in a ponytail. "Okay, you're right. We do have some good ones to choose from." She turned to Pete. "Do you want to read it, or should I?"

Pete took the first book from her hands, opened it to the marked place, and cleared his throat. Then he straightened his shoulders and jutted out his chin. Charlotte thought it was adorable, and she could see from Dana's eyes that she did too.

"'To Be One with Each Other,' by George Eliot," Pete read.

What greater thing is there for two human souls
than to feel that they are joined together
to strengthen each other in all labor,
to minister to each other in all sorrow,
to share with each other in all gladness,
to be one with each other in the silent unspoken memories?

Dana patted Pete's arm. He smiled at her and then lifted his eyes to Charlotte, peeking over the top of the book, waiting.

Charlotte guessed that was the end of the poem, even though it was short. "Oh, I like that." She offered a short clap. "I especially like the part about silent unspoken memories. As the years pass, marriage has a lot of those."

"I'll read the next one. It's my favorite even though it's a little long." Dana scanned the page and then she sighed, just as a painter would sigh when he came upon a brilliant sunset.

"'Love Is a Great Thing,' by Thomas à Kempis," Dana read.

Love is a great thing, yea, a great and thorough good.
By itself it makes what is heavy light; and it bears evenly
all that is uneven.

Dana looked up. "It goes on, but I especially like this line:

Though weary, it is not tired;
though pressed, it is not straitened;
though alarmed, it is not confounded;
but as a living flame it forces itself upwards and securely
passes through all.
Love is active and sincere, courageous, patient, faithful,
prudent and manly.

She ended with a smile.

"Hey, I like that last word. *Manly.*" Pete stuck out his chest.

Dana laughed and patted his flannel shirt. "Yes, I know you do." She kissed him on the cheek, and he blushed slightly. "You've said that the last three times I've read the poem."

"And I'll say it a hundred more if each time gets me a kiss."

This time it was Dana who blushed.

"And what's the third?" Charlotte asked. Although she enjoyed this moment, seeing the happy couple, she had a journal that was waiting. She'd read some, and she couldn't wait to read more.

"Okay, here's the last one." Dana lifted the book close. "'Wedding Prayer,' by Robert Louis Stevenson."

She glanced up, and Charlotte nodded, urging her on.

Lord, behold our family here assembled.
We thank you for this place in which we dwell,

for the love that unites us, for the peace accorded us this day,
for the hope with which we expect the morrow,
for the health, the work, the food, and the bright skies that make our lives delightful;
for our friends in all parts of the earth. Amen.

Dana shrugged. "Sort of simple, but Pete likes it."

"Yeah, because I can understand the words, and because it says we're thankful for food, which I always am."

"Hmmm, let me think about it." While Charlotte at first focused on the couple before her, soon her thoughts turned to Bob and all the years they'd spent together, and she couldn't help but smile. But then, as the last poem was read, she also couldn't help but think of two others from the past. Peggy, who had lost her great love, and Lavina, whose love was tested more than Charlotte could imagine.

From the beginning, when Charlotte had thought of clearing her granddaddy's name, she'd thought about how he must have felt to be accused. How he felt when he lost his job. How he felt when Sunday came around and he knew the only reason the friends and neighbors he cared about weren't meeting in a church was because of him.

She hadn't thought much about her great-grandmother until now. What had Lavina thought? Was it hard to believe in her husband and stand by his side? Had she blamed him? Had she become a better person, a stronger believer in God, because of all she had lost? Had her friends turned their backs on her? Had she ever thought about giving up and walking away?

Charlotte glanced at the Bible and journal. She hoped they both held some answers.

"I don't know," Charlotte finally said. "I think you could use all three. Perhaps Pastor Evans can pray the wedding prayer sometime in the ceremony. And maybe the one by George Eliot could be on the program." Her voice trailed off. "And the other one, 'Love Is a Great Thing,' I think maybe that one should be kept until the first time you have a fight or you wake up and wonder what you've gotten yourselves into."

Both Pete and Dana gave her a blank stare, as if she'd just told them the moon *was* made of green cheese and they'd be traveling there to get some to go with their green eggs for supper.

Then Dana turned to Pete. "Yes, that's a good idea. I do like the idea of this one for the program and this other one for a prayer during the ceremony."

Charlotte noticed that Dana didn't say anything about the second poem—the one that talked about being worried, tired, and pressed. Pete didn't comment either, but as Charlotte watched, he pushed that poetry book to the side, keeping it separate from the other books. Maybe he wanted to read it again later, or maybe he was taking his mother's advice to heart. Either way was fine. Charlotte smiled and then waited for them to leave. She had reading to do, and she was eager to get started.

Charlotte knew she'd share the journal and Bible with her family sometime, but not today. Today it would just be her and Lavina. She was looking forward to getting to know her great-grandmother even better.

Chapter Thirteen

For the second time in two days Charlotte poured herself a cup of coffee and settled down to read. The house was quiet. Sam was out. Emily was with Andrea. Christopher was with Dylan. And Pete had just left for town with Bob to catch up with the guys at AA Tractor Supply while Dana met up with her mom and cousin to go over wedding plans.

Charlotte took her coffee and the journal into the living room, settled onto the couch, placed an afghan over her lap, kicked off her slippers, and opened the journal to read.

November 1, 1880

Everything has changed. Yesterday we sold our building and business in town. Then Elijah put everything we have into buying 240 acres from the Union Pacific. The cost was three dollars per acre, with no down payment. The contract required only the payment of interest for five years, at which time the full payment comes due.

Elijah believes this is a fine deal. He thinks we'll be able to use what money we have to stock and improve the farm, and at the end of five years we can borrow enough to pay off the railroad contract. My fear is that we'll work hard but at the end the railroad will get a developed farm. I try not to worry, but it's hard not to. After all, things don't always work out as one hopes.

Charlotte ran her fingers over the script, trying to picture the woman as she wrote the words. Did she cry or had she already accepted the facts of what was happening? Great-Grandma Lavina's words were simple, not sentimental, but they held so much meaning. Charlotte pursed her lips, wondering if she would respond so graciously, so lovingly, if she were in the same situation. More than anything, she hoped she would. She sighed and turned the page.

July 17, 1881

Yesterday I was pleasantly surprised to have Mr. and Mrs. Vance Ashley call on me. I remembered their faces, but I couldn't place where I knew them from. Mr. Ashley reminded me that Elijah had helped them—must be five years ago now. They were headed west on a wagon train when their wagon overturned while they were attempting to cross Heather Creek after a heavy spring rain. Once they mentioned that, I remembered them. Elijah had given the man his own extra pair of shoes and a set of clothes. He'd also paid for the postage for the man to send a note back to his parents, stating they were returning home to resupply.

Today, Mr. Ashley handed me ten whole dollars, stating he could never repay my husband's kindness. I tried to refuse the gift, but the couple wouldn't think of it. It seems they eventually made it out west, struck a vein of gold in

Montana, and determined the first thing they wanted to do was return and move some of their family members out to live with them. They also wanted to thank my husband for his kindness and stopped along the way. They were sad to hear that Elijah was up in Harding visiting with the bank. The young couple was curious about why Elijah wasn't postmaster anymore and why we were living so far out of town. Mr. Ashley said it took two days just to find us.

My explanation? "Things have changed and we felt more comfortable in the country." He didn't press for answers, and I didn't give them.

The truth is, never in my life was I so happy to see ten dollars. One thing Elijah didn't know before he left is that I am expecting our second child. I chose not to tell him until he returned. I didn't want him to have to worry about having a wife and two children to support. Though deep down I know the Lord provides, I will wait to tell him until after I hear about getting the loan. Then we can truly rejoice over this good news.

Charlotte paused her reading. She knew it was her grandfather, Albert, that Lavina had been pregnant with. Charlotte thought of the generations: her grandfather Albert, her father William, herself, her children, her grandchildren.

If anything had been different, maybe none of them would be here now. Charlotte thought of the movie *It's a Wonderful Life*. It had been her father's favorite film to watch at Christmas, and the more she thought about it, the more she understood why he loved it.

Surely Lavina never understood the magnitude of that one life growing inside her. Charlotte wished she could go back in time to tell the woman, *What you are doing matters. You matter.*

She took a sip of her coffee and moved to the next page.

July 18, 1881

Mr. and Mrs. Ashley left, and the first thing I did was head into town for supplies. Elijah doesn't like me riding alone—especially with Henry sitting on the saddle with me, but I was eager to get to town, pay down our bill at the general store, and purchase a few things, like cloth for a new dress. I'm hardly in my third month, and the waist of my dress is already getting tight.

Mrs. Gilbert was there, and oh, how she plied me with questions. She asked me about my mother and father in the old country. She told me she missed my songs at church. The truth is, I miss it too. I just don't feel as comfortable now getting up in front of everyone to sing. Whenever I see someone looking at me, I always question if they're thinking about the lost money. We go to church often, but it's not like before. Everything has changed.

Henry is almost two now, and I've never heard a little one talk so much. He is nice company, especially after the way Elijah has withdrawn. If I told my husband once I told him a hundred times that I know he didn't take the money. Yet whenever I say it, he looks in my eyes, and I know what his gaze says. He wonders if I think he could have done things differently.

I'm sure my gaze does not lie. Of course he could have. He could have gone straight home instead of stopping by nearly each neighbor's house to tell them of the late train. To tell them it had been delayed a day. Sometimes I wonder if the bag got left in one of those homes. For the life of Elijah, he can't remember if the bag made it home or if he lost the bag along the way. Or if someone took it while he stopped to rest at the church site. Elijah said he stopped to chat with the workers building the wooden foundation of the building.

He doesn't remember dozing off, but I can imagine he did. That man can sleep through any thunderstorm. He's done it a number of times. The pounding of nails to him would be as soothing as a lullaby. My guess is that while he dozed someone took the bag, even though my husband thought he remembered taking it home and putting it in the safe.

Then again, why am I bringing it up now here? I love him, and I'll always love him, no matter what. I have to simply accept the fact that it's up to me to help us find the best situation I can. So Elijah and I will save every penny, make our plans, and trust the good Lord knows best, even about situations we can't understand.

Charlotte tucked the journal under her arm and hurried to the kitchen counter where she'd left her clue notebook. She turned to the page with all her notes and added on:

- Elijah stopped by most of the neighbors' homes to tell them the train had been delayed by a day. (Lavina's journal)

Charlotte tapped the eraser of the pencil against the counter as she thought of something else. She read the entry again, noting that Lavina had written about her husband stopping to rest at the church. What did that mean? Did he lean up against a tree next to the newly built foundation? Did he take a nap in the middle of a field next to the building site? She wished she could put the pieces together.

Charlotte made a mental note to talk to Anita about it. And maybe Maxie. They were both old-timers who'd grown up around the settlers—people whom everyone in town considered part of the historical landscape.

There were many entries, and she mostly skimmed them, but there were some that stood out more, and now she read those.

August 5, 1881

I attended church today. There is a cottage organ that some fine person donated to the congregation. Eloise McHenry played nicely, and I enjoyed singing. At least once after every sermon someone stops me and asks if I miss singing on the stage. I do, but New York City seems like a thousand miles and another lifetime ago.

Charlotte leaned back in her chair. She remembered her mother having a beautiful singing voice—something she hadn't inherited. Yet Charlotte didn't realize her great-grandmother had been a singer too.

September 9, 1881

The church was crowded, and there wasn't a dry eye in the house at the funeral of Gregory Strickle today. I expected to find Peggy in a puddle of tears when I arrived, but instead she just sat on the bench closest to the front in stone silence. I've never seen such a sad face. Her broken heart was evident in her sallow cheeks, and her silence was worse than any tears.

Charlotte placed a hand over her chest. "Dear Peggy," she muttered, making a promise to go back and read in detail about Peggy and Gregory's romance in those letters she still had. At least she could do that much. If no one else remembered or cared, she would.

Charlotte skimmed a few more entries and then stopped on one that made her sit straighter in her seat.

September 17, 1881

I attended church today. Alone. Elijah was out with the cattle feeding, and I couldn't bear to stay inside the lonely house with just Henry any longer. At church there was an old, visiting preacher. Never saw the man a day in my life, but as soon as his sermon was over he approached me with arms spread wide, as if I were his long-lost sister. He was a tall man and twice as wide as Elijah. I don't know what came over me, but I folded into his embrace. He prayed a simple prayer and then held me back at arm's length. Then he said the strangest thing. "What you seek will be found."

I'm not sure if anyone else heard, but I knew immediately what it was. We all would have known.

It's the one thing we've never stopped seeking, yet deep down I have a feeling it won't be found in my lifetime.

Finally, Charlotte turned to the last entry, wiping a tear from her eye.

September 19, 1881

I've kept myself at arm's length from others because I've assumed that everyone in town believes, like the court, that Elijah is guilty. Today my heart is warmed again. I hadn't been planning to go to town, but I needed sugar to make a surprise cake for Elijah. On my way I saw what appeared to be a community barn raising. There were a dozen men building a small house out of real lumber. It was at the Strickle place, and Peggy waved me down. She was actually in the mood to talk today. She asked how our crops were doing. She told me her parents were coming for a visit, something she was excited about.

I haven't been off my farm much and had no idea that Peggy's little sod house had caved in not long after her husband's death. Gazing out in the field, I spotted Gregory's plow still in the furrow. Seeing that made me grateful for what I have. For some it seems we've lost much—our role in town, our business. Our reputation. Heaven knows that rumors about us have sprouted up like the wild grass on the Nebraska prairie.

But as I see Peggy's mourning, I better understand how blessed we are. We have our health. We have our children. And mostly, Elijah and I have each other. Speaking of which, I have dinner to get on the table. He's had a hard day in the field, and tomorrow there's a special prayer meeting at the church. I just might mention to him the thought of us going.

Chapter Fourteen

Charlotte wrapped her hands around her mug and took a sip of cold coffee. *How long have I been sitting here?*

She glanced at the clock, amazed that over an hour had passed. It seemed as if she'd sat down just five minutes ago.

As she was rising to put the cup in the kitchen sink the phone rang.

"Hello?"

"Hey, Mom. It's Pete."

"Hi, Pete. What's up?"

"Oh, nothing much, but I was wondering if you could come into town. I could use some help."

Charlotte looked out the window at the gray landscape. "Your old truck didn't break down in town, did it? I told you to ditch that clunker years ago."

"No, Mom. It's nothing like that. It's just that there's a friendly debate going on, and I need your input."

"Really? Your dad's not giving you any trouble is he?"

"No, I left him at the tractor supply while I hurried over to taste some cakes, but it hasn't been a quick stop. I'm calling from Dana's cell phone. We've spent thirty minutes already arguing over cake flavors. There are four of us, and we're split down the middle. We need you to be the deciding vote."

"What if I don't like either one?" she quipped, again feeling a tug of sadness that she'd never had the pleasure of helping to plan a wedding. And that she wasn't even asked to bake the cake.

"Honestly, Mom, when have you ever disliked something Mel made?"

"You're at Mel's Place? Well, of course you are. She's the best. I'll be right down." Charlotte glanced toward the laundry room, where the pile of clothes was spilling out the doorway. "Well, almost right down. I need to throw in a load of laundry before I head out the door, but that will take only a minute."

"Hurry. If I have to take another bite of either of these cakes I'll be on a sugar high."

Thirty minutes later Charlotte was sitting at one of Mel's tables eyeing the two plates of cake Mel had set before her. Everyone circled around her.

Charlotte moved her fork to the lemon cake, glancing at Dana. Dana watched Charlotte, but her expression gave away nothing. Then Charlotte looked at Michelle, Dana's cousin from Harding, and Dana's mother, Bonnie. Still no hints of who was voting for which cakes.

The cake was lighter than she expected and the hint of lemon brought a smile to her face. It was flavorful and refreshing, unlike any wedding cake she'd ever tasted. "This is nice. I can't believe I've never had it before. It's good. Really good."

"Okay, next is the marble cake." Melody pushed the plate in front of her.

Charlotte took a sip of her water and then took a bite of the marble cake. It was good too—sweeter than the lemon cake. "I like the mix of chocolate and vanilla. It's a wonderful contrast."

She paused. "And while I think either choice would be wonderful, I'd have to go with the lemon."

In an instant arms were around her. Dana pressed her cheek against Charlotte's. "Thank you!"

Charlotte patted her arm. "I suppose that's your choice?"

"Yes, and I have to say, you have great taste!" Dana laughed. Then she turned and high-fived Michelle.

"I think Charlotte knew." Bonnie offered a playful pout. "Everyone knows how much Dana likes lemon anything."

"I didn't, but I do now." Charlotte winked.

"Gee, Mom, thanks for picking the other side." Pete readjusted his John Deere cap on his head. He shrugged and offered a shy grin to his soon-to-be mother-in-law. "Maybe I'll get marble cake for my first anniversary."

"Or maybe your tenth," Bonnie commented, "if you're lucky. Dana can be quite persuasive when she wants to be."

"Well, maybe I can have a groom's cake—in the shape of a carburetor or a cow pie," he chuckled.

The bell on the glass door of Mel's place jingled, and their group instinctively turned to see who had just walked in.

Charlotte felt her stomach tense when she saw it was Sam and that girl—what was her name? Kendall. Sam had his arm around her back, but dropped it as soon as he saw his family sitting across the room.

"Sam!" Pete opened his arms wide. "Dude, you're five minutes late. Man, I needed you." He strode forward and slapped Sam's shoulder. "You like chocolate and vanilla, don't you?"

Sam shrugged and glanced at Charlotte with his eyebrows cocked in a question. "Yeah, I suppose so."

Pete turned around to Dana. "Why don't we try again—two out of three?"

Dana held up a cake order form. "I don't think so, mister. The paperwork's already done." She pushed the order into Mel's hands. "See, it's official now."

Kendall eyed Pete and then turned to the others. "Is that cake?" She moved over to the table. "I love cake." She stretched her hand to Charlotte. "I know Sam was rude and didn't introduce me, but I've been askin' him to. I'm Kendall. Mmmm, that smells good. Like lemons."

Charlotte shook her hand. "Well, you're welcome to taste some cake if you'd like."

Kendall took one of the small forks that Melody used for tasting and dug in. She took a bite and then shrugged. "It's okay. Not very sweet." She took a bite of the marble cake next and smiled. "This one, for sure."

Pete didn't say anything. Instead, he straightened his shoulders and gently elbowed Dana.

"Well, Kendall. I'm going to have to tell all your teachers to dock your grade for not liking lemon," Dana said.

"Gee, Miss Simons. If you dock my grades any more they won't let me in school." She wrinkled her nose. "Except for my photography class. I know I'm acing that."

Dana and the girl chatted for a few minutes.

While they were distracted, Charlotte approached Sam. "Do you want some cake?"

"No, thanks."

"When were you going to introduce your friend?"

Sam tossed his skater bangs. "I was gonna get around to it. It's no big deal. It's not like we're dating or anything."

The bell on the door jingled again, and Charlotte was surprised at the large scowl gracing her husband's countenance as he walked in. Bob fixed his gaze on Pete and then pointed to his watch.

"Oh, man. I completely forgot." Pete slapped a hand against his forehead.

"Yeah, you did. I've been waiting down at the tractor supply for the last hour. Brad finally wanted to close up shop so he offered me a ride."

"Sorry, Dad. It was cake wars. You should have seen it."

Noticing that everyone was distracted, Sam motioned to Kendall and headed back to the door. "Hey, guys, I'll see you later. I promised to get Kendall home before dinner." He offered a slight wave and then was gone.

"Dinner." Charlotte clucked as she looked at her watch.

"Nothing planned?" Melody asked.

"No. I've been reading that journal all day. Remind me to tell you about it tomorrow."

"Sure. I can't wait." Melody adjusted her apron. "I do have some homemade split pea soup on the stove. Homemade bread too."

Charlotte turned to Bob. "Want to eat in town tonight? I have nothing planned and it's Valentine's Day."

Bob sniffed the air and smiled. "I'm always game for Mel's cooking, but what about the kids?"

"Emily's at a friend's house. Christopher too. And Sam..." She looked toward the doorway. "He didn't say what he was up to. I suppose if he's home before us he could make himself a sandwich or something."

Charlotte turned to the others. "Do you want to join us?"

"Actually, I need to get home," Michelle said.

"Yes, and I told Mom I'd eat with her tonight since I'm in town." Bonnie gave both Pete and Dana a quick hug. "Thanks for inviting me to the tasting. It was quite entertaining."

"How about you kids?" Charlotte turned to Pete and Dana. "Do you have big Valentine's Day plans?"

"Nope." Dana answered. "We decided we wouldn't really celebrate this year with the wedding coming up."

"So would you like to join us for dinner, then?" Charlotte asked.

Within a matter of minutes, Bob and Charlotte were sitting at a table across from Pete and Dana, and Melody was serving them some steaming bowls of split pea soup.

After saying grace, Bob was the first one to bring up the sighting of Sam and his new friend. "Who's the girl? I can't say I've seen her around here before."

"She's new," Dana commented, blowing on a spoonful of soup. "I think they've been here less than a year."

"You know, it's sort of weird, but she sort of reminds me of Denise." Bob scratched his head.

Charlotte tucked her hair behind her ear. "Bob, I need to show you some family photos when I get home. Have you forgotten what your daughter looked like?"

"No," he said sternly, his face turning red. "I said she *reminds* me of Denise—not that she looks like her."

Dana tilted her head. "That's weird, because I thought

that too. Maybe it's her smile." Then Dana turned to Charlotte. "I'm sorry, I'm not trying to side against you or anything, but it's weird that I had the same thought. What do you think, Pete?"

"Yeah, sort of, I guess." Pete shrugged.

"Yes, well, I'll have to pay attention next time. And you say they've been here less than a year? I could tell she wasn't from around here." Charlotte took a bite of her bread, making a note to herself that she hadn't made bread in a while and probably should.

"How can you tell that?" Dana tilted her head, her spoon stopping halfway to her mouth.

"Well, I haven't seen too many kids around here dressed like that. Her clothes look like ones I threw out twenty years ago." Charlotte shrugged. "I mean, she has a pretty face and all, but it looked like she went into the closet of a seventies hippie and put on layer after layer."

"I don't know. I think she's kind of cute with those, uh, slipper shoes." Pete rubbed his chin.

"She was wearing slippers? In the winter? She'll catch her death of cold." Bob's voice rose.

"She's like a hippie." Dana put her spoon down. "It's like the seventies but with designer duds."

"She seems like a free spirit to me," Melody said as she filled their water glasses. "I see her around a lot, even during times when I believe she's supposed to be in school."

"Have you met her family?" Charlotte asked as she slathered her bread with butter. "Rosemary told me some things, but it wouldn't be right to repeat them." She bit her lip. "But I will say that I'm not sure I approve of all the time Sam is spending with her."

"Are they the ones who live in that converted bus in the Sunset Mobile Home Park near the edge of town?" Pete asked.

Bob nodded. "Oh, yeah, I remember meeting her dad before. They're a little different. I've seen that guy around, always asking questions about where the old homesteads were and asking about the old dump."

"Just because they live in a converted bus doesn't make them weird." Dana touched Bob's arm.

"Yeah, maybe they're just big on recycling." Pete chuckled.

"I don't know." Charlotte pushed her bowl of soup back, suddenly not hungry. "I just have a feeling that hanging out with that girl isn't the right thing for Sam."

No one else commented, and Charlotte was glad. She hoped she wouldn't have to explain herself. She'd had the same concerns when Denise started dating Kevin Slater—mostly that she'd been so secretive, just like Sam was being secretive about Kendall. With Denise she'd butted in too late.

Not this time. Charlotte rose to go pay the bill, determined to talk to Sam about Kendall. Sam hadn't brought up his friendship with her, and Charlotte hadn't found the right time to ask, although that would be changing. She'd have to *make* the right time. She hated the thought of Sam heading down the wrong path with the wrong person.

This time I'm going to say something before it's too late.

CHARLOTTE DIDN'T HAVE to wait long to talk to Sam. She and Bob had been home only ten minutes and were still warming themselves before the corn-burning stove when Sam entered.

"Hey." He nodded his chin toward his grandparents, kicked off his shoes, and moved toward the stairs.

"Sam, not so fast. Your grandma and I want to talk to you."

"About what? I did all my chores. And my homework. Actually, I, uh, honestly don't have any homework tonight."

Bob settled into his chair, and Charlotte moved to the sofa. She sat and folded her hands on her lap, saying a quick prayer for guidance. Sam sat beside her, perched on the edge of the cushion.

"I'm not worried about your homework. Your grandma and I are more concerned with who you've been keeping company with lately." Bob turned to Charlotte. "What's that girl's name?"

"Kendall," Sam said before Charlotte had a chance to respond.

"Yes, well, what your grandfather is trying to say is that we worry she's a bad influence."

"I've heard she doesn't go to church." Bob said. "And then there's the matter concerning her parents. We haven't seen them much in the community." Bob cleared his throat.

"They're not like typical Nebraska folks." Charlotte tried to make her voice as soft, as kind, as possible.

"What's wrong that? And for your information it's not *parents*. She just lives with her dad. Have you met him, or are you just repeating stuff you've heard? Gee, Grandma, you're always talking about how Mrs. Cunningham likes to poke her nose into everyone's business. Now look at you."

"Sam, that's no way to talk to your grandmother." Bob leaned forward and gripped Sam's arm, and Charlotte noticed his nostrils flare. Charlotte patted Bob's hand, trying to calm him.

Sam didn't respond. Instead he turned and looked at the kitchen door. His foot tapped a double beat.

"Actually, there is some truth to that. I've never met these people." Charlotte blew out a breath. "It's just, well, you must be aware of how things look. Kendall misses a lot of school. It seems like everyone around town knows that. In fact, I saw you driving around with her during school hours the other day. And her family. Sam, you're being so secretive about your relationship. Do you think Kendall is a good influence on you?"

Sam sat there, staring at his hands, and at first Charlotte wasn't sure if he'd heard her.

He shrugged. "She's just a friend. It's not like we're going to run off and get married or anything. Besides, there are a lot of cool things about her you don't even know. You haven't even given her a chance," he snapped.

"That's enough. I'm not going to stand for your tone of voice." Bob pointed toward the stairs. "We'll finish this conversation when your attitude changes."

Sam slumped off, and Charlotte pushed her hair back from her forehead, reminded again how hard this parenting thing was.

Charlotte waited until she heard Sam's bedroom door slam shut. Then she turned to Bob.

"Do you think we're being too hard on him?"

"I don't think so. We do have concerns, and I think we

needed Sam to know that." Bob rose and took his glass to the kitchen sink, rinsing it out.

"I suppose the thing I'm worried most about is Sam's plans for the future. He was talking a lot about college, and I haven't heard anything about it recently. The more I think about it, I wonder if Sam was just making those plans for Arielle—you know, to look good in her eyes."

"Could be. It wouldn't be the first time a boy tried to impress a pretty girl." Bob winked. "In my opinion, if that's what it takes, then so be it. That's all right with me. Doesn't always matter what the motivation is, just that it points him to the right path."

Charlotte rose and moved to the kitchen. She took a peanut butter cookie from the cookie jar and broke off a piece, even though she wasn't hungry. "I suppose that's exactly what I'm worried about. What is Kendall all about? If she's skipping school herself, I wonder if she's going to encourage Sam to do the same."

"I suppose we'll worry 'bout that when the time comes. Maybe you're right. No use staring up at today's clouds and worrying about tomorrow's rain."

Charlotte took a bite of the cookie and slowly chewed. "Yeah, suppose not."

She stood there, eating the cookie but not really tasting it. She thought for a minute, wondering if she should bring up the same worried feelings she'd had with Denise. *Maybe I should have been worrying about tomorrow's rain back then.*

Bob clicked on the television, and Charlotte guessed the conversation was over. She considered heading upstairs and talking to Sam, but did she really think he'd listen to her? She was just an old grandma. What did she know?

She thought about asking Pete for advice but realized that was out of the question. Pete was getting married in a month. He was up to his neck in wedding stuff.

She glanced over at Bob, who was now shouting letters at Vanna White.

Maybe I'll talk to Pastor Evans about it when I'm at church tomorrow. I'll take advice wherever I can get it.

Charlotte thought of another common saying that her mother often used: "It's better to nip it in the bud." Sam hadn't done anything wrong yet. And it was better to deal with it now than wait, wasn't it?

It couldn't hurt to talk to Pastor Evans about it, right?

Chapter Fifteen

Emily felt like she was going to throw up or faint or maybe do both as she entered Lily Cunningham's house, tagging behind Andrea and Mr. Cunningham. It was different than she expected. Friendlier. Warmer. The carpet was rose-colored and a large, comfortable-looking floral sofa sat in front of the window. Photos of Lily and her brother, Jason, hung on the wall. In the photos Lily had a big smile, something Emily hadn't seen too often around school.

"Mom, I'm home," Andrea called.

"In the kitchen," Mrs. Cunningham replied. "Grandma's here too. Come in, Andrea. I'd love to introduce Emily to her."

Emily kicked off her shoes by the front door where the other shoes were lined up. "Uh, where do you want me to put my bag?" Emily looked around. The whole house was perfectly clean, and she didn't want to mess it up.

Andrea skipped toward the kitchen. "Just leave it there. We'll get it later," she called back over her shoulder.

Emily set it on the floor and then followed Andrea into the kitchen.

"Grandma M!" Andrea gave an older, round woman a large hug.

"Emily, I'd like to introduce you to my mother, Mrs. Marley," Mrs. Cunningham interrupted.

Emily extended her hand. "Hello, Mrs. Marley."

The older woman took Emily's hand and shook it politely. "None of that Mrs. Marley stuff. Call me Grandma M. Everyone does."

Emily shrugged. "Uh, okay."

Mrs. Cunningham motioned to the dining room chair next to her. Emily sat.

But instead of sitting, Andrea hurried to the fridge, and began rifling through it. "Want a peanut butter and jelly sandwich?" she asked.

"Uh, sure," Emily said.

"Only one." Mrs. Cunningham wagged her finger in Andrea's direction. "You don't want to spoil your appetite. We're having fried chicken for dinner."

"Fried chicken. My favorite!" Andrea whooped.

Emily stiffened in the chair. She hadn't even thought about telling Andrea she was a vegetarian and didn't eat meat. The last thing Emily wanted was to make a scene at the table. She'd heard her grandma talking about Mrs. Cunningham before. If you told the woman anything you could be sure that the whole town would hear about it by the next afternoon.

Even though they were just relaxing in their home, Mrs. Cunningham seemed like she was ready to walk out the door in her red pencil skirt and black sweater. And, Emily noticed, Lily's grandmother was even more put together. She wore a long skirt and a bright orange blouse. Her earrings matched her outfit, as did her necklace and nail polish. Emily thought of her own grandma, who wore jeans and sweatshirts most of the time. Even though at the beginning, when she'd first moved to Nebraska, Emily had wished her grandma took more time with her appearance, the way she dressed made sense to Emily now.

"So you girls don't have any Valentine's Day plans?" Mrs. Cunningham asked.

The girls let out a collective groan. "Please," Andrea said. "We are trying to pretend that it is just any other day."

"Well, that sounds fine to me," Grandma M said. "I think Valentine's Day is highly overrated."

Emily was surprised and happy to hear that. She had been a little bummed that she didn't have a boyfriend to celebrate the day with, so in a way coming to the Cunninghams was a good excuse to forget about it altogether.

"Where's Lily?" Andrea asked with a mouth full of sandwich. Amazingly Mrs. Cunningham didn't seem to notice or care.

"She's at violin lessons. We've started up again. You know, for a while she was quite bored with it—being the best musician and all—but her father insisted that she keep going. He said that in all of life we need to adjust to people who aren't quite as talented as we are. Owen thought it would be a nice growing experience for her."

"Of course. Who doesn't love the violin?" Grandma M took a sip from her teacup.

They chattered on about a zillion different topics over the next fifteen minutes. Emily knew that Mrs. Cunningham talked a lot, but she was an amateur compared to Lily's grandmother. Grandma M shared gossip about nearly every family between Bedford and Harding, scarcely taking a breath. Most of it didn't seem to matter. I mean, who really cared that Pastor Evans got a flat tire and had to call a tow truck? Or that the principal of the elementary school was seen exiting an all-you-can-eat buffet in Harding last Friday night?

Still, Emily waited and listened, wondering if the conversation would come back to her family. It did.

"You know . . ." Mrs. Cunningham turned to Emily. "I was talking to Lily the other day, and she told me that Sam has a new girlfriend."

"Well, I wouldn't really say they're dating." Emily shrugged. "They're friends, that's all."

"Hmmm. . . . I heard it's much more than that, but I suppose you know better than I, my dear," Mrs. Cunningham said.

"Who are her parents?" Grandma M asked, pouring herself another cup of tea from the china teapot, which looked old but didn't have even one chip in it.

"I'm not sure. I haven't met them. I just know Kendall from school."

"Kendall." Mrs. Cunningham's penciled eyebrows arched. "That's an interesting name."

"I've never heard of a girl named Kendall before. Maybe it's a family name. So. Are the wedding plans going well for your uncle and Miss Simons?" Grandma M switched conversations quicker than one flap of a hummingbird's wings.

Andrea looked at Emily and held back a chuckle.

Emily ignored Andrea and thought of the conflict she'd had with Dana concerning the wedding dress. Everything was fine now, but it had been a hard couple of weeks. Still, she didn't want to tell these women that.

"Oh, yes. I think everything's going good. My grandma's just happy that Uncle Pete found such a nice girl."

"That's nice, dear. I'm sure her wedding dress will be lovely."

"Yes, it is, and the cool thing is that I'm designing the bridesmaids' dresses," Emily said. She didn't know why, but she had a strange desire to please this woman.

"You?" The woman pinched her lips together as if trying not to smile. "That's unique."

"Yes, I suppose it is." Emily shrugged, not knowing what else to do or say. She had to admit that she also found it funny that she was talking like they did. Talking like a middle-aged woman having tea.

"Yes, well, Miss Simons is lucky to find your uncle Pete. I heard that she's been engaged two times before—you know, when she was away at college, but I'm not sure if I believe that. I hope this one sticks. I heard her mother saying the other day Dana would have a simple but happy life with Pete."

Simple? Emily didn't like the way the woman said that word—as if simple were the same as boring or unsatisfactory. Her grandparents had a simple existence, but their lives were anything but boring.

The conversation turned to the new computer Mr. Cunningham was buying Lily for her birthday.

Emily quickly ate her sandwich, wiped her mouth, and then stood. "Thank you for letting me come over. Andrea and I better get to our school work now. We have a lot to do."

Andrea motioned for Emily to follow, and as soon as she left the kitchen Emily released a slow breath. She followed Andrea down the hall.

"Are they always like that?"

"What do you mean?"

"I mean, do they always talk about everyone and everything? And do they always talk that quickly? I was having a hard time keeping up with who was doing what with whom and why."

Andrea opened the door to a bedroom. It was large, and there were two twin beds against the walls. One bed was perfectly clean, and painted wooden letters hanging above it spelled out L-I-L-Y. The second bed was hard to spot under the piles of clothes, books, makeup, and other stuff.

"Isn't everyone in America like that? I mean I thought all families talked and talked and talked."

Emily moved to Andrea's bed and pushed aside some things to sit. "No, not really. I mean, my grandma probably talks the most, but sometimes my grandpa goes through a meal hardly saying anything. Sam sometimes stays quiet too. I mean—"

The door swung open, and Lily entered with her violin case swinging in her hand. She was smiling, but as soon as she saw Emily her smile faded and she stopped short.

"Hey, Lily." Emily offered a quick wave, and her stomach knotted up. She thought about asking about violin practice, but that sounded stupid. She then thought about mentioning what they had found at the library, but she didn't want Lily to think she'd only come to work. Instead, she just sat there, waiting for Lily's response.

"Oh, hi. I forgot you were coming over." Lily looked at Emily. Then she turned to Andrea. "Hey, I was looking for my red sweater—you know the one you wore last week. I couldn't find it in your clothes pile."

Andrea didn't seem to mind Lily's curtness. She pointed to the closet. "That is because Mom came in and took out the dirty clothes. I saw it hanging on your side."

Lily opened the closet. "Oh. I just wasn't expecting it to actually be put away."

"Hey, Lily, do you want to watch a movie with us later?" Andrea approached her sister, her smile in direct contradiction to Lily's frown.

"I don't know. I might not be here."

"But if you are?" Andrea didn't miss a beat. "We'll watch something good."

"Yeah, fine, whatever."

In the large walk-in closet, Lily had what looked like a sewing table. Emily stood to take a better look.

"Wow, I really like your sewing machine." Emily forced a smile as she eyed it, hoping the whole night wouldn't be as awkward as this. Unlike Grandma's old sewing machine, it had all types of buttons and levers.

"Grandma M gave it to me for my birthday last year. I swear that woman is intense. The year before she gave me a guitar. And the year before that a video camera. If I show one bit of interest in something, she thinks I'll be the best ever at it. But I do like to sew." Lily tugged the red sweater off the hanger and slipped it on.

"Me too."

"Yeah, I remember. You made that really cute shirt that one time."

Emily paused, surprised by the kind words coming out of Lily's mouth. She remembered Lily's comment. It had been the one time Lily had seemingly been nice to her.

"My grandma's not like that at all," Andrea butted in. "She doesn't ever think about what I like. Instead, she buys me strange things." Andrea sat on the floor with a flourish.

"Like what?"

"One time dishes were on sale, and she bought them for me. She says they are for when I am married, but I've never even had a boyfriend! My mom says my grandma is like this because of how she grew up and everything was so expensive. Now she buys things because they are not expensive, even if she doesn't know what to do with them."

Emily still eyed the sewing machine, checking out the various buttons. "I suppose I never thought about that before." Emily turned back to Andrea. "My grandma buys sale stuff too—mostly food, but that's because Sam eats like a horse."

A snicker burst from Lily's lips, catching Emily by surprise. Her cheeks reddened slightly, and Emily wondered what that was about. Emily was going to make another comment about Sam, just to get Lily's reaction, but more words spilled from Lily's mouth before Emily had the chance.

"My mom says my grandma is the way she is because she grew up on a homestead and had nothing," Lily explained. "She lived in a soddie and only had one dress.

The other kids teased her so she always has to look nice now. I think she's trying to be perfect because she never wants to be teased again. Not only that—she wants my mom and me to be perfect too."

"Lily?" The voice caught all three of them by surprise, and they all turned toward the open door. Lily's grandma was standing there. She wore a smile, but it looked as if it had been ironed on her face. Her eyes appeared downcast, and Emily was sure Grandma M had heard at least part of Lily's comments.

"Lily, dinner is ready. Your mom told me to come get you."

A sick feeling rushed over Emily, and she wrapped her arms around her stomach.

"Uh, okay."

"Unless you're not hungry." Grandma M tilted her head.

"No, we're coming."

Grandma M nodded and then turned back toward the kitchen. Emily released the breath she'd been holding. Lily didn't say anything, but Emily could tell from her face that she felt bad about the comment. And, for the first time ever, Emily wished she could actually do something to help Lily.

They ate dinner in the dining room, and thankfully no one commented when Emily ate only salad and mashed potatoes. The conversation around the table was pleasant, but Emily could tell that Grandma M was watching her words more carefully than before. She even brought up a story about when she'd tried to sew a dress and she sewed the sleeves on backward and had to throw it away—maybe to prove that she wasn't perfect after all.

Afterward, the three girls worked on posters that showed some of the first train routes across the Great Plains. During the evening they cracked jokes, and Lily seemed different than she did at school. Nicer.

After they'd done enough homework for the night they watched *The Princess Diaries*—one of Andrea's favorite movies. The only time they weren't all together was when Grandma M left and Lily walked her to the door. Yet when Lily came back she didn't have a happy look on her face. Instead she sat quietly on the couch, chewing on her fingernails as she watched the movie. Emily wondered if Lily's grandma had said something. Or if something else was bothering her. Emily looked at Lily from the corners of her eyes and suddenly felt sorry for her. She couldn't imagine living in a household where everyone expected you to be perfect all the time.

When the movie was over, the three of them lined up in sleeping bags across the living room floor. Emily wasn't sure how, but she found herself sleeping in the middle.

The room was dark. The house was quiet, and Emily could hear Andrea shuffling around in her sleeping bag.

"Do you two have many of the same classes?" Andrea's voice sounded like it was beginning to fade.

"We do, I guess," Emily said. She waited, thinking of what else to say, and wondering if Lily would comment.

"You should study together more often." Andrea yawned.

Neither Lily nor Emily said anything. Emily knew the main reason they didn't hang out or even talk very much was Nicole. From the first time she met Nicole Evans, it seemed, the preacher's kid had been out to get her.

"Yeah, maybe. That would be nice. And maybe sometime you could both come and spend the night," Emily answered.

"Well, I did stay the night once." Lily shuffled around in her sleeping bag.

Emily leaned up on one arm and turned toward Lily, even though she couldn't see her in the dark. "Yes, I remember. It was last summer when Shae Lynne was in town filming that music video."

Emily chewed on her lower lip, remembering how horrible that sleepover had been. With her grandmother's encouragement she'd tried to forgive Nicole for the conflict in the past, but it had turned out to be a complete flop when she caught Lily and Nicole making fun of her room and her clothes.

"Maybe the next time will be a better experience," Emily said.

As she lay there, she thought about how angry she'd been when she walked into her bedroom and heard Lily and Nicole talking about her. The hardest thing, though, was the fact that she'd been *trying* to be nice. She had tried to forget the stuff from the past and start over. It just hadn't worked that way.

But now, as she lay in the dark, Emily realized that Lily was different than she'd thought. There was a hidden part of Lily she hadn't known, a part she wished she could see more often.

"Tomorrow I will sing you a Czech song," Andrea announced.

Both Emily and Lily chuckled.

"Okay. Uh, is there any reason why?" Lily asked.

"It's a song about a train. Maybe we can use it." Andrea's voice was no more than a mumble.

Emily patted Andrea's head. She smiled even though she knew Andrea couldn't see it. "What a great idea. A song about a train in a language that no one in the class can understand. It's *exactly* what we need."

Andrea answered with a snore, and Emily heard the slightest giggle coming from Lily.

"Emily." Lily's voice was no more than a whisper.

Emily turned her head slightly. She tried to see Lily's face, but all she saw was darkness.

"Thanks for being Andrea's friend."

"Yeah, sure."

Emily waited for more, but there was only silence. She wanted to say something to Lily about standing up to Nicole—standing up about allowing Andrea to join their group and everything else—but she didn't. Things were going well. Emily didn't want to mess it up. "Good night, Lily," she said instead.

"Good night."

Then Emily snuggled down to go to sleep.

The day had been completely different than Emily had expected.

Better.

Chapter Sixteen

Charlotte pulled her jacket tighter around her neck and patted her leg. "Come on, Toby, keep up," she called without looking back. The air was cold on her face, biting her nose, yet the sun slightly warmed the top of her head. It was one of the nicest February days they'd had so far, and Charlotte wanted to take advantage of it. She'd spent enough winter days cooped inside. It felt good to get outside and breathe in the fresh air. To walk the gravel road. To stretch her legs and let her mind think over everything she'd learned about her granddaddy so far.

The crunch of car tires and Toby's bark met her ears simultaneously. Charlotte glanced over her shoulder and realized she recognized the car. Toby must have recognized it too and had trotted down the road alongside it.

Charlotte turned and waited, waving to Dana. Dana didn't wave back. She pulled up next to Charlotte, her hands gripping the steering wheel. Charlotte opened the door and noticed the tear streaks on Dana's face.

"Want to give me a ride the rest of the way home?"

Dana nodded but didn't answer.

Charlotte suddenly felt sick. She hoped she hadn't done anything to upset the girl. More than that, she hoped Pete hadn't done anything.

Toby wagged her tail next to the open door. "Do you mind if Toby jumps in too?"

"Sure. That's fine." Dana attempted a smile. "I like Toby. In fact, maybe Toby should come to the wedding."

Charlotte patted her leg, and Toby jumped in squishing between the dashboard and Charlotte's feet.

Dana drove the quarter mile home in silence. It was only after they parked and went inside that Charlotte dared to ask what the problem was. She walked to the sofa, turned to her side, and patted the cushion next to her. As Dana plopped down beside her, Charlotte asked, "Do you want to tell me what's going on?"

"It's my mother. She's trying to do everything—take over everything." The words spilled from Dana's lips like water from a faucet. "She asked months ago if she could help address envelopes. I told her that would be great. Then yesterday before the cake tasting she asked for more invitations. I don't have more invitations. They were expensive, and Pete and I only got enough for the ones on *our list*."

"Are you saying there's another list?" Charlotte took Dana's hand in hers.

"Yes, *my mother's* list. She knows everyone in all of Adams County, and she thinks they all need to come. I looked it over, and out of about one hundred people I probably recognized ten names."

Charlotte considered how to respond. Personally, she knew how hard it had been to pare down her own list—after all, she and Bob had lived in Bedford their whole lives. They knew everyone in town, and most of those people had watched Pete grow up. She was sure they could fill Bedford Community Church to standing room only. Yet it had been Pete and Dana's choice to have a small ceremony with only family and a few close friends.

"Well, perhaps—" A knock at the door interrupted Charlotte's words. She looked up to see the door open and Hannah's smiling face peering in.

"Anyone home?" she called.

"Oh no! I look a mess." Dana wiped her face. Then she rose and hurried to the bathroom. "I'll be right back."

Charlotte stood and glanced at her watch. It was barely 9:00 AM. She forced a smile on her face as she motioned Hannah inside.

"What are you up to this morning, Hannah? Out early I see."

"Yes, well, I saw the sun peeking through the clouds, and I thought I'd pop over and see if you wanted to walk. I thought about calling, but I didn't want to wake the whole house up."

Charlotte moved to the kitchen, pulling a mug from the cupboard. "Oh, Bob, you know, has been up for hours. Christopher and Emily are staying at friends' houses, and Sam . . ." She cocked her head as if trying to listen for him upstairs. "I haven't heard a peep out of him. He's usually out doing chores by now, but we had some words with him last night, and I'm wondering if he's decided to hide away for the day." She set the coffee cup on the counter. "Would you like a cup? It's fresh."

"Of course. Sitting over coffee is just as good as going for a walk." Charlotte heard the squeak of the bathroom door.

Hannah moved to the dining room and sat down. "I'm not interrupting anything, am I?"

"No, Hannah, you're fine." Dana sniffled into a tissue. "I was just crying on Charlotte's shoulder. It seems my mother has hijacked my guest list, and I don't know what to do."

"Yes, well, I'd say your mother is one of the most sociable people I know. She was always on one committee or another when she lived here, and I'm sure nothing's changed."

Charlotte poured Dana a cup of coffee too and handed it to her. "I'm sure she doesn't want anyone's feelings to get hurt."

Dana sighed. "I know, but she has no idea what a big wedding costs. She and Dad gave us a small amount of money, and Pete and I are trying to stay within our budget. I'm digging into my savings too. I just don't like the idea of starting our marriage off in debt just because my mother wants to stay in good graces with the Rotary members."

"I can imagine. I remember staying up to watch Charles and Diana's wedding. What year was that?" Hannah combed her fingers through her hair, as if trying to stir up a memory. "Oh, yes. 1981."

Dana leaned over to Charlotte and smirked. "Before my time."

"Hush now." Charlotte playfully swatted her arm, happy to see Dana's spirits had lifted.

"Did you see that wedding, Charlotte? The reporter said there were thirty-five hundred people there. That's bigger than Bedford! Oh, and the dress," Hannah rattled on. "I've never seen a prettier wedding dress—not even when Karilee Hamlin married that Foster boy up at that big mansion in Harding."

"I don't even want to know how much that royal wedding cost," Dana muttered. "But the money isn't the point. It's my day, and I want to celebrate it with those I know and love best."

Charlotte settled down in the chair next to Dana and added a spoonful of sugar to her coffee, stirring it slowly. "You know, maybe there's a way to compromise," Charlotte suggested. "Can you give your mother a limit—such as twenty extra friends—and then ask her to donate more for the cost of food and everything else? I imagine if you showed her your budget and shared your struggles—just like you did with us—and explained your heart, then she would probably understand and be willing to cut down her list."

Dana rested her chin on her hand. "You're right. I suppose I just need to talk to her."

"She's excited." Hannah sat on the other side of Dana and wrapped her arm around her shoulders. "Her little girl is getting married. I know if I had a little girl I'd want the whole world to come to the wedding."

"Thanks, Hannah." Dana wiped her face. "You've got me crying again. And maybe . . ." She looked toward the window. "Maybe I need to be a little more understanding too."

She turned and winked at Charlotte. "I'll tell her she can invite *24* guests—an even number, you know."

They chatted over coffee a while longer, and Charlotte enjoyed hearing more about the wedding plans. "You know," she offered, "if there is anything you need help with, be sure to let me know."

Dana's face brightened. "Really? I appreciate that. You know I do need help with the favors. I'm still trying to come up with something unique."

"I can help too," Hannah piped up. "I never mind putting in a little elbow grease."

"You can talk to my mother for me," Dana quipped.

Hannah's face fell. "Well, I . . ."

"Just kidding." Dana patted Hannah's hand. "I wouldn't do that to you."

Through the window, Charlotte spotted a car coming down the driveway. The old, yellow Volkswagen pulled to a stop in front of the house. Charlotte's jaw dropped as she noticed Sam getting out of the car.

"Oh, my word." She braced herself against the counter.

"Is that Sam?" Dana rose and hurried to the window.

"I thought you said Sam was upstairs sleeping?" Hannah also rose and moved to the window. "Who's he with? I've never seen that girl before. Is that Sam's girlfriend? She's kind of cute!"

Charlotte crossed her arms over her chest and turned her body toward the door. Sam waved good-bye to Kendall and then opened the door. He paused as he noticed three faces staring at him. For a moment it looked as if he were going to bolt up the stairs.

"What's up?" Sam kicked off his skater shoes and hung up his coat.

Charlotte approached him. "What do you mean, what's up?" She lowered her voice and leaned close to his ear. "Sam Slater, where in the world have you been? It's ten in the morning. I thought you were upstairs sleeping."

Sam pulled a small white bag from his cargo pants pocket and thrust it into Charlotte's hand. "It's a cinnamon roll from Mel's. I know how much you like those."

"You were at Mel's?" Charlotte felt her heartbeat slow from its wild pounding.

"Yeah. That's not against the rules, is it?"

"When did you leave?" She glanced back over her shoulder and noticed that Dana and Hannah had moved back to the table and were attempting to have their own conversation. Charlotte was thankful. There was nothing harder than parenting with an audience.

Sam leaned one shoulder against the door jam leading into the laundry room. "I don't know. A while ago."

"Like last night?" Charlotte's heart skipped a beat.

"No. Grandma, please. It was this morning."

"Is that all you're going to tell me? There's nothing else you want to tell me?"

"Not really. I promised I wouldn't." He pulled his work jacket off the hook. "Except that I'm going to head out and get to my chores now."

Charlotte stepped away from the door and watched as he hurried out. Then she turned her attention back to Dana and Hannah, trying to remember what they'd been talking about.

Suddenly the worries about guest lists and cake options didn't seem important. Sure, she wanted to help Pete and Dana have the best day possible, but more than that, she wanted Sam to make good choices—to think about the decisions he was making. To consider the company he kept.

What in the world could he be doing this early in the morning that he promised not to tell me about?

Chapter Seventeen

Saturday afternoon found Charlotte at the church again. Nancy Evans had planned another work day—this time on the weekend for those who couldn't make it during the week. Charlotte was there for the cleanup, but she'd come for another reason too. Instead of heading to the basement, as soon as Charlotte entered the church she turned toward the pastor's office. The door was partly ajar, and Charlotte stood there and questioned if she should bother him. Pastor Evans was most likely busy preparing for tomorrow's sermon.

Changing her mind, she turned and almost ran into Nancy. "I was just coming to ask Nathan a question. Did you need to talk to him?"

"Yes, well, I do, but I can do it another day."

Nancy waved her hand in the air. "Nonsense. No use waiting. Come on in. Being a pastor isn't about the sermons, you know. It's about the people. Nathan will be the first to tell you that."

Nancy swung the door open, and Charlotte followed. The pastor was on his computer, his fingertips clicking the keys. He glanced up and paused as they entered. "Hey, what's up?" He stood and gave his wife a quick hug and then shook Charlotte's hand. "How's that basement looking? Last time I was down there I couldn't believe how much had been done. We have some mighty women in our church." He chuckled.

"The work's going well," Nancy said. "That's what I wanted to talk to you about. Do we still have that Women's Group meeting Monday morning to make plans for the open house?"

His eyes widened, and Pastor Evans softly struck his forehead with the palm of his hand. "Oh yes, I forgot about that. Thanks for reminding me. I need to announce that in church tomorrow." He jotted a quick note and stuck it on his computer screen.

"Great, that's all I have." Nancy smiled and moved toward the door. "But I think Charlotte has something else she wants to talk to you about."

"Sure, sure, Charlotte. Why don't you have a seat?"

Charlotte sat, and Pastor Evans leaned forward, his gaze upon her. She glanced at his computer and then back to him. "Are you sure? If you need to finish up, I can come back another time."

"No, I have a few minutes. So what's happening?"

Charlotte folded and unfolded her hands. "The truth is, pastor, it's about Sam. There's this girl he's been spending time with—someone Bob and I don't approve of. Actually, it's not so much the girl I'm worried about. It's just the way he's been sneaking around, like he's up to something. I was wondering if you could give me some advice."

"Me?" Pastor Evans sat straighter.

"Well, as you know, his dad really isn't in the picture," Charlotte hurriedly said. "And Bob and Bill are more intent on telling everyone what needs to be fixed than having a two-way conversation and listening. Then there's Pete. He and Sam usually get along great—he could probably give me advice—but he's swept up with all the wedding plans. I'd like to talk to Sam, but I don't know what to say. I'm afraid I've already started off on the wrong foot with him concerning this Kendall girl. I think he sees me as too quick to make a judgment and not open enough to getting to know her or understand."

"Well, are you?"

"Am I what?"

"Open to getting to know the girl." He leaned back and rested his arms on the chair.

"I guess so. I'd like to be. It just seems like they're being secretive." She stroked her chin. "I suppose we could invite her over to dinner sometime."

The pastor nodded once. "Good. I think that's a good start, and I appreciate your willingness to try. I wish I would have had someone like you around when I was Sam's age. I'm not sure if you know much about my past, but my high school and college years weren't my proudest moments. I made a lot of bad choices. Had to learn the hard way."

"Some of us do." Charlotte thought of Denise. "But it's good to see those people come back around."

"Yes, well, I almost didn't."

Charlotte tried to hide the surprise on her face. "Actually, I don't know much about your past.... I was just trying to think of someone who could give me advice about Sam. I'd never want you to talk about something you're not comfortable with."

Pastor Evans chuckled, and then he rose and walked to the window. "Oh, I don't mind talking about those years. For my shame and God's glory. I think it's the members of the congregation who have a hard time hearing about them. The senior saints—those older than you."

Charlotte shifted in her seat.

"You see, unlike Sam, I was raised in a Christian home and spent every Sunday and every Wednesday night in church. The problem was that when I hit high school my school friends seemed cooler than my church friends, and I focused on hanging out with them. We vandalized property. We stole stuff from cars and even from houses that we found unlocked. We found ourselves in all types of trouble. When I was seventeen, I was arrested for shoplifting. When I was eighteen, I was kicked out of school. My parents didn't know what to do with me. And at nineteen—well, my whole world came crashing down when my best friend died."

He glanced up at Charlotte, and she could see that he was getting emotional. "We were spray-painting on a bridge, and he slipped down an embankment. I heard him land. It was horrible. He cried out for me, calling to me to help him, but he was dead by the time I got to him."

Now it was Charlotte who was trying to control her emotions. She dabbed the corners of her eyes with her fingertips. "I don't think Sam is that extreme."

Pastor Evans raised his hands out front as if defending himself. "I wasn't suggesting he was. I just wanted to encourage you in your role. There's a good chance that Sam will make a mistake—maybe even a big one. But remember that even if he does, the story doesn't have to end there."

Charlotte nodded and stood. "Yes, of course. Thank you. I appreciate that." She thought about Denise. Even though she'd had a rocky start to adulthood, her daughter grew up and changed, becoming a responsible mom and a lovely woman. Charlotte swallowed hard. "Thank you for your time." She turned.

"Charlotte?"

Hearing her name, she turned back around.

"I just have to say one more thing before you leave." He paused as if trying to figure out his words. "Sometimes we try to protect our kids too much. Sometimes it's the difficult stuff in life—the hard knocks—that brings us closest to God. There are things I've done, and things that have happened to me, but through those times I've discovered that God's always there. I've learned life is not just about following a list of rules; it's about knowing Jesus every step."

"Thank you, pastor." Charlotte crossed her arms over her chest and thought again about her great-grandparents. They had never planned on life turning out the way it did for them, but Charlotte could tell from what she was learning about them that they had drawn nearer to God, even during the hard stuff.

With quiet steps Charlotte made her way to the basement. The laughter of women met her ears as she entered, and she said a silent prayer, thanking God for putting her family in this community of believers who cared for and supported each other.

Chapter Eighteen

Charlotte was surprised when she walked in the front door of her house and found Emily in the kitchen.

"Hey, I thought you were going to give me a call when you needed a ride. I even tried to call the Cunningham house earlier, but no one answered."

Emily shrugged. "Yeah, we've just been running around town all day. Lily has her license now, and she gave me a ride. We stopped by Kepler's to get poster board and markers. Lily had the coolest idea. We're going to re-create one of the advertising posters the railroad used to post, but we're going to translate it into English. Andrea already translated the words for us. I can't wait for you to see it, Grandma. They made Nebraska sound like it was the Promised Land."

"I think it *is* the Promised Land," Charlotte answered.

Christopher jogged down the stairs.

"How did you get here?" Charlotte asked. "I thought you were at Dylan's."

"Yeah, I called and you weren't here, so Grandpa came to pick me up. And guess what?" Christopher hurried over to her. "Dylan and I decided we want to help you figure out the case of the missing money. That's what we're calling it. He already talked to his mom, and we're going to the library after school on Monday.

"Also, we saw Mr. Barnes from the newspaper, and he said he was going to follow up with a reporter at the Harding paper to see what sort of records they have. Maybe they'll carry my story too."

Uneasiness settled over Charlotte like a cold fog. Just when she'd become okay with the idea of having her granddaddy's story printed in the local paper, here it was possibly expanding beyond their town.

"That sounds wonderful, Christopher. It will be nice to get the help, but I have a feeling that I'm getting close to running out of information. The more I think about it, the more I doubt that I'll ever be able to solve what happened to the money. The good news is that I know more about my great-grandparents. I know what good people they were and how they were respected by the community."

Christopher nodded, but she could see he was only half listening. "Do you mind if I look at your clue book?" He held up a notebook. "Dylan thought it would be a good idea if we had our own notebook with our own notes."

"Sure. Just don't go running off with it." Charlotte tapped the side of her head. "My memory isn't as good as it used to be."

Christopher hurried over to the desk where Charlotte kept her notebook.

Charlotte took lettuce and other produce from the fridge. She'd put in a pot roast before leaving for the church. Now she only had to make a salad to go with it.

"Christopher, can you please set the table after you finish jotting down those notes? You know how Grandpa likes to have dinner ready when he comes in from the barn."

"Uh-huh." Christopher took a seat at the desk and began copying her notes.

"Grandma." Emily placed a hand on her hip. "I was talking to you, and Christopher totally interrupted. I wasn't done telling you about our history project."

Charlotte tried to remember what Emily had been talking about before Christopher had come down the stairs. "Oh, you're right, Emily. I'm sorry." Charlotte apologized. "I did want to talk to you about the sleepover at the Cunninghams' house. How did it go?"

"Well, it was good. Andrea is really nice. I like her. She's really funny. Especially when she's tired."

"And Lily? Did you get along with her?"

Emily took a carrot from the cutting board, leaned against the counter, and nibbled on the end of it. "She was fine. I mean, we're still not the best of friends, but we got along. This morning she showed me a shirt she's sewing that is cool."

"Good. Maybe she'll actually talk to you at school."

Laughter burst from Emily's lips. "Uh, I don't think so. As long as Nicole is around, that's not going to happen."

As Charlotte cut up the lettuce she thought about her interaction with both Pastor Evans and his wife, Nancy, today. Did they know how difficult Nicole was?

Christopher was still writing at the desk. Emily pulled some glasses from the cupboard and began setting the table. Charlotte could see from the look on her face that the reason most likely had something to do with still wanting to talk rather than the fact she was helping her brother.

"Grandma?"

"Yes, Emily."

"Have you ever met Mrs. Cunningham's mother?"

Charlotte thought about it for a moment and then shook her head. "I think I've seen her a few times, at school functions and stuff, but I can't really say that I've met her. Was she nice?"

"Yeah, I suppose so. She was nice to me, but she had something to say about everyone else in town."

"Really. Now I know where her daughter gets it."

"Yeah, that's what I was thinking."

"I guess we follow what we see," Charlotte mused.

"That makes sense." Emily pulled plates from the cupboard. "It's strange, though, you know."

"What's that?"

"Well, once I met her grandmother and mother, I sort of understood Lily better—why she is like she is."

Charlotte wanted to jump in and ask more questions, but she just nodded and continued to chop the lettuce into tinier and tinier pieces.

"It must be hard when everyone around you expects you to be perfect." Emily let out a soft sigh. "But the cool thing is that we're supposed to meet over here next week to finish up the project. That's okay, isn't it?"

"Of course it is. I'm eager to hear it. You're going to practice on me, right?"

"Sure, and—"

"Oh, Emily," Charlotte interrupted and then hurried to

the desk. "There's something I thought would be helpful in my great-grandmother's journal. It's about the railroad and land sold."

"Wait. You actually have *your* great-grandmother's journal? And it has information on settlers and the railroad? How come you didn't tell me?"

Charlotte's jaw dropped, and she tried to remember if she had mentioned the journal when she was talking at the dinner table or to Bob. Maybe she had only mentioned it once. She was just glad that Emily was interested in it now.

"May I read it?"

"Yes, anytime. Just make sure you put it back here when you're done so it doesn't get lost."

Charlotte heard Sam's feet pounding on the porch ten seconds before he entered the house.

"Hey, you." Charlotte tried to sound nonchalant. "What have you been up to?"

It wasn't until he'd walked all the way into the kitchen, slamming the door behind him, that Charlotte noticed Sam's pants.

He shrugged. "Oh, you know. Just hanging around with my friends."

"In the middle of a mud bog?" Charlotte shook her head. "Don't you head upstairs." She pointed to the laundry room. "Strip down in there. Some of your sweatpants are folded on the dryer."

Emily walked by Sam, taking the extra silverware back to the drawer. As she walked by, her face contorted. "Oh, yuck!" She opened her mouth and pinched her nose. "What's that smell?"

Charlotte sniffed the air. At first all she smelled were the wonderful scents of pot roast. Then she scooted closer to Sam, and the stench hit. He smelled like rotten chicken, dirty diapers, and mildew all mixed together. "Sam Slater, what on earth have you been in? Did you fall into the sewage pond?"

Sam lifted his arm and sniffed his sweater. "I don't smell that bad."

"Yes, you do!" Christopher called from where he sat at the desk. "I can smell you clear over here."

The door opened, and Bob entered. He took one step in and then stepped back out. "Charlotte, what in the world are you cooking for dinner? Whatever it is, throw it out now!"

Charlotte waved him inside. "Bob, get in here. You're letting the cold air in. And it's not dinner you smell; it's Sam."

Bob walked in, holding his nose. "Sam, did you die and come back to life or something? Boy, you stink."

Charlotte grabbed a wooden spoon off the counter and then pointed it at Sam. "Strip down and change your clothes."

"Fine." Sam staggered into the laundry room. A minute later he reemerged in his sweats.

"Where have you been?" Charlotte asked again. She steadied her gaze on him.

"Yeah, I haven't seen you all day," Bob echoed, taking off his boots, hat, and gloves.

Sam tossed his hair out of his eyes. "Well, I was with Kendall. Don't give me that look, Grandma. We were with her dad too. He's really cool. In fact he told me I could invite you guys to come along sometime. I told him Christopher would especially like it."

"Where were you? What were you doing?"

Sam bit his lip. "I can't really tell you. Of course, if you come with us then you'd see for yourself."

"You can't tell us?" Bob's brows folded. "I'm sorry, Sam, but in my book anything that's a secret is something you shouldn't be doing."

"Fine. I'll tell you. It's not a big deal. We weren't doing anything wrong. We were at the old dump site south of town with the metal detector. Just don't tell anyone, okay? If word gets out that we're finding treasure then everyone's going to be out there searching."

"The old dump site? Isn't that still in use?" Bob asked.

"Yes, but we hiked down to where it was in the beginning. Hank finds all sorts of coins and stuff down there."

"Hank? Isn't that a little informal?" Charlotte carried the salad to the table.

Sam shrugged. "He asked me to call him that."

"Is that what that girl's dad does for a living? He goes around with an old metal detector and tries to find treasure?"

"Not really treasure. Just old stuff. He's a nice guy."

Bob walked in his stocking feet over to the dining room table, pulled out a chair, and sat down. "That may be true, but even nice guys have to put food on the table. I bet that's why they live in that bus—he doesn't want to get a real job."

Sam's eyes looked from Charlotte to Bob and then back again. "Are you guys being serious? I can't believe this. I can't believe what's coming from your mouths."

"Sam," Bob said sternly, and they all knew it was a warning.

Sam crossed his arms over his chest. "Sorry, Grandpa," he mumbled. "But really, maybe you should get to know them."

"I know that Kendall doesn't attend school very much. Both Melody and Dana said so," Charlotte spouted. Her chest constricted, thinking of the type of people Sam was getting involved with. *Why can't he see the problem? It's the people we spend time with who influence us the most.*

Sam sighed. "Why don't you ask her about it? Have you thought of that?" He turned and walked off. "There might be a good reason."

"I sure hope so," Charlotte mumbled under her breath. Even though she understood what Pastor Evans had said, she hoped Sam didn't have to learn the hard way.

Chapter Nineteen

The church fellowship room seemed extra warm this afternoon—mostly from the wall heaters turned on high, but perhaps also from the excitement that came from the women who were coming toward the end of their group project.

Charlotte settled into the women's ministry meeting, pulled off her coat, and glanced at her watch. She just hoped the meeting didn't last too long. Emily, Andrea, and Lily had gone to Mel's Diner to meet up with Ashley, and then Charlotte was supposed to take them back to the house for dinner and help them work on the project.

Mary Louise Henner sat down next to Charlotte, setting sheet music on her lap. "I hope this doesn't last too long. It's my day for practicing my organ pieces." Her brows knitted together. "If I don't practice this one hymn I might just have to cancel for Sunday."

Charlotte patted Mary Louise's hand. "I need to slip out early too. If we're not done in twenty minutes we can slip out together."

"Welcome, ladies." Pastor Evans strode to the front of the room. "First of all I wanted to start by thanking you for all the hard work you've put in. When Nancy and I first came up with this idea I never expected that we'd have everything done by February 28, the 130th anniversary of the first service that took place in Bedford Community Church, but you did it. Give yourselves a hand."

Charlotte clapped with the others, but it felt silly, really. It was just cleaning and organizing—something they were used to doing everyday.

When the applause died down, the pastor continued. "My idea for this meeting is that we figure out how we should organize the display case. Also, we need to discuss which items are most important to include."

"Why don't we start by sharing some of the items we've found?" Nancy interjected. "There are so many good things. Maybe if we pick a few we can better know how to set up the display case."

"Good idea." Pastor Evans placed a hand on his wife's shoulder.

"I found an old handbell." Stacie Lindstrom waved her hand. "There's a date on it from 1883, and from the research we found at the library it most likely was the bell that Mabel Olsen, one of the first Sunday-school teachers, used to call her students to class."

Murmurs erupted around the room, and Charlotte loved hearing the excitement in people's voices.

"Wonderful." At Pastor Evans's words, the room quieted again. "Anything else?"

Mary Louise Henner stood. "Yes, well, in one of the boxes Celia Potts and I found a folder of sermon notes from one of the first preachers in our church."

"Yes, and the sermons were quite good. Maybe you should read over them, Pastor," Celia spouted.

Charlotte placed a hand over her mouth and shook her head. It wasn't the first time she'd been shocked by Celia's lack of tact.

"I imagine the sermons *are* interesting," Pastor Evans commented, amusement lighting his face, "but I'm not sure how well they'd work for a display. I don't think people would want to stop and read them. Still . . ." He smiled. "I'd be happy to take a look."

"What about Charlotte's find?" Nancy piped in. "Well, actually I was the one who found the items, but they have to do with Charlotte's family."

"Yes, Charlotte." Mary Louise jabbed Charlotte in the ribs with her elbow. "You should talk about the Bible and journal and the story about your great-grandfather."

Charlotte looked from Mary Louise to Nancy to Pastor Evans. "I don't know. Like the sermon notes, they really aren't something that will work for the display."

"No, I imagine not, but Nancy's told me bits and pieces. I'd love to hear about it if you'd like to share." Pastor Evans motioned for her to stand.

"Well, what I found isn't like these other people's items. In fact, at first I wished the newspaper clipping hadn't come up at all." She took a breath. "I'm sure many of you heard that in 1879 the money set aside to buy the building materials for this church was either lost or stolen while it was in the care of my great-grandfather. I'd heard the story before, but I didn't know much about it. In our searching through the boxes, Hannah found a newspaper clipping and Nancy found my great-grandmother's Bible and journal. But more than that, I found something too." Charlotte clasped her hands together in front of her.

"You see, at first I was curious about the truth. Then I felt ashamed. It's almost as if I felt people looked at me differently because of what my great-grandfather did."

"No, Charlotte," Maxie mumbled. "Surely you didn't think that."

Charlotte cast Maxie a soft smile and then scanned the group. "But through some letters Anita shared with me, and some photos from Maxie and then the journal, I found something that I didn't expect. I—"

"Did you find out what happened to the treasure?" Mary Louise called out from the back of the room.

Charlotte shook her head. "I didn't figure that out, but I discovered something even better. I learned that even though my great-grandparents went through hard times they were good people. I learned that friends can come alongside you and make all the difference. I also learned that it's okay to still have joy, even when others judge you without knowing the truth." Charlotte paused as she replayed her last sentence in her mind. Then she sat down immediately as the face of Kendall popped into her mind.

No, that's a different situation. She tried to ignore the gnawing in her gut.

She glanced at her watch again and then rose, happy that she had an excuse to leave.

"Going somewhere?" Pastor's voice interrupted her pace.

She paused and turned. "Yes, I have some girls to pick up. They're working on a school project. I'm sorry to run out like this." Her voice didn't sound like hers; it sounded tight, unnatural. She hoped no one else noticed.

"Yes, I understand. I think Nicole has the same project due soon, but Charlotte, before you run out can you commit to sharing the story you shared with us, maybe on the day of the open house? You're right that those items won't work for the display, but the history of the place—and the love of the people—is something we need to hear."

"Are you sure? I don't want to distract from the main point of the program—you know, the celebration of the founding of the church."

"Well, your family's story is part of the church's story." Pastor Evans spread his arms wide.

"Yes, I suppose it is."

CHARLOTTE NOTICED THAT Lily sat quietly in the front passenger's seat as Emily, Andrea, and Ashley chattered in the backseat. Charlotte's car was small, and they were squished, but they didn't seem to care.

"Ashley, that's awfully nice of you to come and help the girls with their project."

"Yeah, well, my group's project is on the food of Nebraska. We met. We cooked. We tasted. We cooked some more. My dad thinks it's an instant A." She laughed. "I mean, it's going to be so tasty. And—"

"Yeah, we aren't going to have food," Emily interrupted. "But I was thinking that we should have something really cool to display."

"These posters will be nice," Andrea said.

"Yeah, I guess." Emily twisted her lips, showing she was thinking. "What do you think, Lily?"

"My brother has a toy train. Or at least he had one. I can't remember if it was made to look old, but something like that would work." Lily's voice was soft, and she seemed respectful, different from the times Charlotte had seen her with Nicole. Charlotte waited for Emily or the other girls to comment. None of them responded, and Charlotte looked toward Lily. Her jaw was tight, and Charlotte could tell she felt uncomfortable, out of her element.

"Emily, did you hear Lily? She made a good suggestion." Charlotte pulled the car onto their long driveway.

"Yeah, I heard. I was thinking about it. I just was thinking of how that could work."

"Hey, what about Miss Middleton's train?" Ashley's voice rose with excitement.

"Who is Miss Middleton?" Andrea asked.

"Oh, she's the cool old lady Emily and I cleaned for last year." Ashley pushed her red, curly hair back from her face.

"Even though I didn't want to at first," Emily explained. "But she turned out to be pretty cool."

"Yes, she was on this thing called the Orphan Train that took orphans who lived in the cities and sent them to be adopted by people who lived in the country."

"How sad." Andrea pouted. "I mean how sad that she lost her parents—not how sad that she was adopted or that she moved here and got a new family." Andrea leaned forward, stretching her arm to pat Lily's shoulder. "Sometimes moving in with a new family isn't bad at all."

Lily smiled, but she didn't say anything.

Charlotte drove down their driveway, and Toby came bounding toward the car.

"Grandma, do you think it would be okay if I called Miss Middleton and asked to see if we could use her train display for our presentation?"

"Sure. I don't see why not. She might even like to come and hear the presentation. And maybe you can have her say something to the class. After all, even though she didn't move to Nebraska until the 1920s she would have known a lot of the people who first settled here." Charlotte turned off the engine.

"Good idea!" Emily bounded from the car. "I think I'll call her now."

SAM SAT NEXT TO KENDALL in the small pickup truck. Kendall's dad was driving. They drove on a road leading out of Bedford and then turned onto a narrow dirt road that Sam hadn't even noticed before. "So glad you're joining us today, Sam. It's always fun to have another treasure hunter in the group."

Sam nodded. "Yeah, thanks for having me. The other day Kendall showed me some of the cool antiques you guys found. We tried to go to one of the sites, but the road was too icy. I'm glad we're able to try again with you." Sam tried to act natural, like he did this every day. But it wasn't easy. His stomach tightened, and his shoulders tensed. "I can't believe most of that stuff came from our area."

The dirt road narrowed until it was no more than two tire tracks leading toward a grove of trees in the distance.

"Yes, most people have no idea what's in their own backyard." Mr. Richardson laughed. "And we don't *want* everyone to know. If people knew what we were up to then we'd be out of work, out of treasure."

"If you say so, Mr. Richardson." Sam felt his stomach tighten more, and he hoped his grandma and grandpa wouldn't say anything about what he'd already told them.

"Please, Sam, call me Hank. I've told you that before." He sighed. "Mr. Richardson sounds like my father."

"Okay, Hank."

The road ended in a small cluster of trees and Hank jumped out. Sam did the same, pulling on a hat and gloves.

"See that small hill over there?" Hank pointed to a hilly area near the farthest tree.

"Yeah."

"That's not a hill. It's an old soddie. You can tell by the size. Hills around these parts are more gently sloped and they're wider."

"So that's where we're going to look?" Sam moved in the direction of the soddie.

"No, Sam, wait." Kendall's voice halted his tracks. "We need to grab our gear first."

"Yeah, sorry. I was getting too excited." Sam turned and saw her lifting the metal detector out of the truck. As Sam took the metal detector from her, an uneasiness came over him that he couldn't shake.

Kendall reached back and grabbed the shovel and pick.

"Uh, Kendall. Is this private property?"

"Yeah, it is. But—"

"Kendall, Sam!" Hank's voice called from up ahead.

"Hurry. We don't have all day. We don't want anyone to see us."

"Coming," Kendall called, hurrying ahead.

Instead of following, Sam just stood there, feeling like a fool.

Why didn't I figure this out sooner? I'm so stupid.

Ever since Kendall started talking about the treasure hunts she went on with her dad, he'd thought it sounded like fun. Up until now he hadn't considered it might be illegal.

Great. What should I do now?

He looked down at the metal detector in his hands. Suddenly he felt unsure about this entire situation and wondered if he should leave...

"Sam!" Kendall called, hurrying ahead. "Come on. We don't have all day."

Sam took a deep breath and followed. "Maybe we won't find anything," he mumbled to himself. "Then I won't have to worry."

DINNER WAS FINISHED and Emily was glad that Grandma had asked Christopher to help with the dishes. Grandma and Grandpa hadn't been their usual cheery selves at dinner, and Emily guessed it was because Sam wasn't home. He was most likely out with Kendall again. No one knew. All Emily knew was that he'd left a note on the counter that had read, "Be back before 9. Will eat when I get back."

Emily took a sip of the hot cocoa Grandma had made

her and tried to focus on the notebook in front of her. Andrea and Ashley were at the other end of the table, working on the posters, and she and Lily were supposed to be working on the presentation. Instead, Emily stared at her notes for a least a minute without really seeing them.

Lily jotted something down in her notebook, but she didn't say anything.

"Oh, my goodness! Andrea, how do you even pronounce that word?" Ashley pointed to a large word on the poster. "Czech must be the hardest language ever."

Excited by Ashley's interest, Andrea launched into an impromptu Czech lesson.

As she sat there trying to concentrate and trying to ignore Ashley's loud voice, Emily suddenly wished she hadn't invited Ashley to come over. She'd felt bad because they hadn't been spending time together, and Ashley had offered to help, but Emily could see now it wasn't a good idea. Emily had just been getting to know the other girls, and Ashley's presence seemed to throw things off balance.

"That's cool about Miss Middleton, you know, letting us take the train to school," Lily offered.

"Yeah, I nearly had to shout into the phone for her to hear me, but when she finally understood, she said it was fine. She also said it was a replica of an old steam engine—the kind that brought settlers to Nebraska, so it fits with our project."

"Too bad she isn't feeling well enough to come too, you know, to tell the class about some of the people she knew."

"Yeah, I hope she's not too sick. She sounded pretty frail on the phone. But I'm going to talk to Grandma later when she's not so stressed about my brother and see if she has any other *really, really* old friends. Maybe there are others we'll be able to interview."

"Yeah, I bet my grandma does too." Lily leaned back in her chair and folded her arms on her lap. "But the last thing on earth I'd do is ask her for help."

Emily frowned. "Why?"

"Are you kidding? If I told her about the project she'd go crazy getting involved in it. She'd hire someone to build a replica of Bedford 1880 for us. She'd sew us period costumes. She'd build a time machine to take us back so we could ride the train ourselves."

Laughter burst from Emily's lips. "Okay, I have to admit *that* would be cool."

"Yeah, I suppose so. But some things don't have to be perfect. I try to tell my mom it's okay to just do a good job without having to make yourself be better—or look better than everyone else."

Emily nodded and didn't know how to respond. Grandma and Grandpa always encouraged her to do her best, but they didn't get crazy about it.

Emily straightened in her seat. "Oh! Oh!"

Lily turned to her, eyes wide. Even Andrea and Ashley turned to her to see what was so exciting.

"I just remembered. My grandma has an old journal that was my great-great-great grandmother's, and she wrote some stuff about the trains."

"Really?" Lily flicked Emily's shoulders. "Well, go get it already. We can use that. I mean, really use that. We can read a journal entry and then describe more of what was happening in the area during that time. It's perfect."

Emily jumped from her seat. "Grandma!"

"In here." She heard Grandma's voice coming from the laundry room. "If you can't find me it's because I'm buried under these piles of clothes."

Emily peeked into the laundry room. Her grandma was bent over with her arm reaching deep into the dryer pulling out warm clothes. "Grandma, do you have time, you know, to show us that journal? The one your great-grandma wrote?"

Charlotte straightened, and her face brightened. A minute ago she had seemed tired, but now her eyes were alert and she smiled.

"Of course. I'd love to. I even went back this morning and put bookmarks on the pages I thought you'd be interested in. I thought about using sticky notes but I didn't want to mess it up. The paper's really thin."

"Cool, well, whenever you're done here, Lily and I would like to look at it."

Emily turned, but her grandma gently grabbed her arm, pulling her into the room. "Is Lily okay? It seems like something's bothering her. She doesn't seem to be her typical self."

"Yeah, I actually don't mind. I don't like her typical self." Emily covered her mouth with her hand. She couldn't believe she'd actually said that out loud. "Oops. I, uh, just think she's not used to us. I think she'll start acting more, uh, normal when she's more comfortable."

Grandma nodded, but she didn't look convinced.

The phone rang and Emily went to get it, but Grandpa was already in the kitchen, staring into the empty cookie jar. He picked up the receiver.

"Hello?"

Emily stood at the end of the kitchen counter, listening in, wondering if it was Sam. Wondering if he was going to get chewed out.

"Oh, hi."

Nope, not Sam.

"Yes, it's good to hear from you. I haven't seen you around church much."

Emily searched her mind, trying to remember who had missed church lately.

"You are? I'm sorry to hear that."

Sorry to hear what?

"Oh, that's good." Grandpa nodded and pulled the phone back from his ear, as if the person on the other end was talking really loud.

"Who is it?" Charlotte sidled up to Emily.

"I'm not sure."

"Really, that's kind of you, Miss Middleton. Okay, I'll tell her. Yes, if she can't do it tomorrow, I can. Yes, it's a quiet time of the year around the farm, but spring is right around the corner."

"It's probably about the train," her grandma said, leaning close.

"Yes, and you too. Good night now." Grandpa hung up the phone.

"That was Miss Middleton. She's already boxed up the train for you. She said her niece insists that she come stay with her for a week or so, and she wants to make sure you get it before she leaves. She said she's leaving at noon."

"But I have school." Emily twirled a strand of blonde

hair around her finger. "Unless you wanted me to miss or something . . . I wouldn't mind."

"I don't think so." Her grandma poked her arm playfully.

"I can get it if you need me too." Grandpa poured himself a glass of milk and drank half of it in one gulp.

"No, I can run into town. I don't mind at all," Grandma said. "A few of us were going to stop by the library and talk to Mary Louise's niece anyway. She was going to show us the pictures she has before she puts them on display. We might be able to borrow some for our 130th anniversary celebration."

"We saw the photos already." Andrea said from the dining room. "They are super." Andrea rolled her *r's* and gave two thumbs-up, making Ashley break into uncontrolled giggles.

"Oh, while you're there, can you pick up some copies she said she'd make for us? It's research facts and stuff for our presentation."

Grandma moved to the desk where the computer sat. "I better write this down. I know I'll forget."

Grandma jotted a note to herself and then went to her china hutch, where she'd left the journal. "Now, girls, are you ready for this? I think you're going to love some of these parts where my great-grandmother talks about being a settler and how the train affected their lives. I found a few references the first time I read it, but I was mostly just skimming. This morning I went back and read more." Grandma smiled. "Some things, I think, will surprise you."

Chapter Twenty

Charlotte could tell something was different about Sam when he walked in the door later that evening. His cheeks were bright red and his ears were too. He was trying to hide a smile, but he wasn't too successful at it.

"Sam, where in the world is your hat?" Charlotte rose from the table where she'd been reading the journal with the girls. "Look at you. If you're not careful you're going to get frostbite."

"Yeah, then they're going to have to cut your nose off. I read that in a book once," Christopher called from where he was doing his math homework on a TV tray by the couch.

"Grandma, I'm fine." Sam let out a heavy sigh.

She sniffed the air. "Well, you don't stink, so I suppose that's a good thing."

She forced a smile, knowing she had an audience. As soon as the girls saw Sam they were no longer interested in the journal or in working on the posters.

"Where have you been?" She folded her arms across her chest.

Sam bit his lip as if he wanted to say something but didn't know how to say it. He stuck his hands in his pockets but didn't take off his coat.

Charlotte waited for him to answer. "Well?"

"I can't tell you. I promised I wouldn't. But . . ." He blew out a long breath. "I can *show* you something if you promise you won't tell anyone." He pointed to the girls at the table. "That includes all of you too."

The girls nodded. Charlotte didn't answer. She didn't like this type of promise, but it didn't matter. Sam acted as if he were going to burst if he didn't tell. He dug into his jacket pocket and pulled out a silver object.

"Is that a woman's hair comb?" Charlotte took it from his outstretched hand and held it up to the kitchen light to get a better look. It had five prongs and had a Victorian tiara pattern. Although it was tarnished it looked like it was made from sterling silver. "Wow, Sam, this is beautiful."

Bob sauntered over and took a look. "I remember my grandma having something like that. Not so fancy though."

"Hank said women used to use these for their hair. He said if I get it cleaned up we can take it to the antiques auction. He told me he's seen one like this go for fourteen hundred dollars before."

"Did you say fourteen dollars or fourteen hundred?" Bob coughed as if the thought of such a thing took his breath away.

"Fourteen *hundred*."

"You're joking," Christopher butted in, peering at the comb to get a better look.

"No, it's an antique. Some people spend a lot of money on antiques."

Bob looked around the room at all the items—on shelves, on the wall, in cabinets. "If that little thing is worth that much money then we need to clean house. Why, we could retire and move to Florida with all the money we could make from this place."

Charlotte chose to ignore his comment. "Sam, do you have anything else?"

He pulled an old spoon from his pocket.

"Let me guess. That's worth two thousand?"

Sam shrugged. "I don't know. Hank's going to look it up tonight. Kendall says he has all types of books on antiques. It's his passion. In fact, that's why they live on a bus. They move into an area, look it over, and then move out. He—" Sam paused and then his eyes grew wide. He pressed his lips together as if he'd said too much.

"Can we see?" Emily and her friends approached, and for the next few minutes they ogled the object.

Ashley held the spoon with her little pinky sticking out and pretended to be eating from an invisible cup of soup. "Where did you find this stuff?" she asked.

"Oh, just in the sewer."

"What?" Ashley opened her fingers as if she'd just been scalded. The spoon dropped to the floor. "Are you serious?" She hurried to the kitchen sink and began scrubbing her hands.

Sam laughed, and then he bent down to retrieve the spoon. "No, I'm not serious. But you'd better be careful. You're going to dent it." He brushed it against his pants.

"Are they yours to keep?" Ashley asked.

Sam frowned. "No. They belong to Hank. I forgot they were in my pocket. He said I'll get part of the profit once I sell them."

The girls watched with interest.

"So, where *did* you get those things?" Charlotte dared to ask.

Sam shrugged.

"I don't know. Someplace."

"You're not going to tell us?" Bob stepped closer. "I don't like the sound of this Sam. It's as if you're hiding—"

"I'm not hiding anything, okay?"

"Well, if you're not hiding anything then you can tell us." Bob stood in front of Sam with his hands on his hips. It was clear he wasn't going to let Sam get out of this one.

Sam lowered his voice. "We went to the Driggers' farm. There's an old soddie on the back forty—or what used to be an old soddie."

He placed the items on the counter and then moved to the fridge. "Got any leftovers?"

"In the red plastic container. Don't reheat it in that bowl though; it will melt." Charlotte looked at Bob, and she could tell he was thinking the same thing she was. This conversation wasn't over yet, even if Sam had tried to change the subject.

"So . . ." Bob walked to the kitchen and leaned back against the counter, crossing his arms over his broad chest. "Did you get permission—you know, from the Driggers?"

Sam dumped the leftover egg noodles into a glass bowl. "Um, I don't know."

"You don't know, or most likely, the answer is no and you don't want to tell us?" Charlotte asked. She turned to the girls and waved them back in the direction of the dining room. As she did, a great wave of fear hit her heart as if someone had taken it out of her chest and dunked it in ice water. She glanced back and realized Lily was here, and she had no doubt that not only would this episode be passed on to Lily's mom, but also soon the whole community would know.

"I don't think that's right. Those things belong to the Driggers. It's their property," she said.

"Not only that, but they could have arrested you for trespassing," Bob added.

Sam put the bowl in the microwave and set the timer for one minute. "Wow, you guys are making a big deal out of nothing. The truth is that the Driggers haven't paid attention to that soddie in twenty years. They just planted around it. Also, the Driggers didn't own the property when the soddie was there. And before that the Native Americans were free to roam the land. Who gave us the right to start taking it away from them, dividing it up, and fencing it off? If anyone has a right to take what they want it's the Native Americans."

"That doesn't make it right."

Sam took his food into the dining room and sat between Lily and Ashley. Then Sam started asking questions about their project and the posters they were making, making it clear that he was done with the conversation.

"Sounds like that *Hank* is feeding a lot of information into that boy's head—more than just information on spoon prices," Bob said.

"Yes, Kendall's family is sure having an impact on Sam. I just don't like it very much," Charlotte answered.

Charlotte thought about what she and Pastor Evans had discussed. Was she being too critical? Maybe she was;

maybe she wasn't. But perhaps it was better to be safe than sorry.

"Humph." Bob kept his gaze focused on his oldest grandson. "How long did Sam say they've lived here?"

"I think he said about a year."

Bob nodded. "That's good. Maybe it means they'll be rolling out of town soon."

Chapter Twenty-One

Charlotte hoped her face didn't look alarmed as Lydia Middleton welcomed her into her house. The woman was just a little-bitty thing anyway, but Charlotte had never seen her so frail.

Lydia coughed, and the motion of it shook her frame. "Hurry in, dear. You don't want to let the cold air in."

Charlotte hurried inside and thought she would be knocked over from the heat. A fire blazed in the old wood stove in the corner and the whole house smelled like dust. Charlotte wondered if Lydia had had any help with the housecleaning after Emily's and Ashley's summer job ended. She doubted it.

"I'm so glad you could come. I was worried about Emily not being able to use the train. I was so excited when she called. She is a dear girl, you know."

"Yes, well, she appreciates you sharing it. She's been working hard on this school project. She's looked up photos and journals from 1880 . . ."

"Eighteen eighty?" Lydia interrupted. "I think I have some letters from that time period." Her small eyes brightened. "In fact, I was cleaning the other day and I came upon them again. Last week when I was dusting, I accidentally dropped our old family Bible. I had forgotten how heavy it is. I'm not as strong as I used to be, and the letters tumbled out onto the floor."

Charlotte's heart skipped a beat as she followed Lydia to the bookcase. Lydia reached for the Bible, and her hand trembled from the weight of it. Charlotte quickly reached to take it from her friend's hands. It was big, but not that heavy. Her concern for Lydia increased. How old was she now? Eighty-nine?

Charlotte opened the front of the Bible. The letters were addressed to Iva Spilko.

"Iva was my mother's best friend. They were neighbors for many years. She spoke with a thick accent, and there were times I couldn't understand a word of what she was saying, but I always understood her hugs and kisses. It did my young heart good."

Lydia's voice was shaky, and Charlotte tried to picture her as a young girl. Was her hair once blonde? Dark? It was hard to tell now because it was white—whiter than Charlotte had ever seen. Charlotte turned over the envelope. "Do you mind?"

"No, go ahead and open it."

Charlotte sucked in a breath as she noticed the date on the envelope: April 7, 1879. *Only one week after the money was lost!*

Charlotte scanned down the page, and the joy emptied out of her as if someone had pulled the plug. "It's . . . it's not in English."

"Oh, yes, dear. I should have told you that. Iva was from

another country. Germany maybe? Her mother was also German, and she lived in Omaha. Iva saved all her letters. When her mother died, Iva was given all her mother's letters too."

"So you have a whole box of them?"

"No. I saw the box when I was younger, but it got lost over time. That's why I was so surprised to find these in the Bible. She must have pulled them out for some reason. Maybe they're special."

"I only wish we could read them."

Lydia scratched her white hair and narrowed her gaze as if she were thinking hard. "Do you know anyone around town who speaks German?"

"Oh, maybe Greta Harbinger. I believe she was born in Germany. Maybe I can bring her over..."

Lydia shook her head. "No, that won't do. I'm leaving, remember. I'm not sure when I'll be back."

Charlotte put them back in the Bible. "I understand. Maybe when you return we can get together."

"Aren't you listening?" Lydia chuckled. "Or maybe it's just me talking when I'm half-tired." She took the letters from the Bible and placed them back in Charlotte's hand. "Take them. It's not like I'm going to need them anytime soon. Ask around, and if you find someone be sure to let me know what they say."

Charlotte placed her hand on Lydia's, "Are you sure?"

"Yes, dear." She turned back to the box with the train. "Oh, I should have asked you to bring Bob or Pete. I'm afraid I won't be able to help you carry that box."

"Oh no, Lydia. Don't worry about it." Charlotte tucked

the letters into her pocket and then lifted the box by the handles. It was surprisingly light, but she didn't let on.

With her hands full, Charlotte lifted her chin to wave as she went out the door. "Please enjoy your time with your niece, and thank you for doing this for Emily. I'll take some photos of the presentation so you can see it."

Lydia offered Charlotte a tired smile. "Thank you, dear. I appreciate it."

Charlotte hurried out to her car, reminding herself that she'd need to return those letters when she returned the train.

For now, she wanted to try to get in touch with Greta Harbinger and see if she'd be willing to take a look at the letters.

She let her to-do list of the day play through her mind: lunch and quilting with Rosemary, grocery shopping, and then a stop at the pharmacy to pick up Bob's prescriptions. Last night she'd remembered that Christopher had set up a time to meet with Mr. Barnes after school, and she was about to cancel her time with Rosemary when Dana had offered to pick up Christopher.

"I'm heading out to the farm to bring some photographers' portfolios," she'd said. "Maybe you can help me get Pete to actually sit down and look at them—so I can get Christopher if you'd like."

Just remembering Dana's kind gesture put a smile on Charlotte's face. Is this what it would be like to have another woman around again? Someone to help share the load? To jump in and offer to help? The idea made her smile.

As Charlotte drove to Rosemary's she realized she hadn't had that type of relationship in a long time—if ever. Denise had left when she was just eighteen, and their relationship after that had mostly been over the phone. Anna was a wonderful wife to Bill, but she and Charlotte had never gotten really close. Charlotte attributed that to the fact that their interests and hobbies were different, and also because Anna's mother lived near to her and was a big part of her life.

Maybe I should invite Dana to the quilting group sometime in the summer when she's not teaching.

Even as Charlotte thought of it she grew excited. Another name to write into the front page of their family Bible. Another heart to graft onto her own.

Chapter Twenty-Two

Dana and Christopher were sitting at the table when Charlotte entered the house with her arms full of groceries.

"Do you need help?" Dana rose from the table and hurried over. Then she motioned to Christopher. "Come on. Let's help your grandma."

Christopher jumped from his chair and approached Charlotte with Toby trailing by his side. "Is there more in the car?"

Charlotte placed the bags on the counter. "Actually, there is. Thank you, Christopher. Thank you, Dana."

Dana shrugged. "No problem." She started emptying the items from the bag on the counter. "He's young and strong, and it's never too early to start training a gentleman."

"Training up gentlemen, yes. I did my best, but I think we could've done better in that area."

Dana opened the fridge and put away the fresh produce Charlotte had just bought. "I don't know. Pete tries to act tough and manly around here, but he does pretty well. He opens doors for me, and last week when he picked me up at school he engaged in polite conversation with some of the other teachers, even though I could see from his gaze that he was completely bored."

Charlotte chuckled. "Better than I'd expect."

Minutes later the groceries were put away and Charlotte was enjoying a cup of coffee from the pot Dana had made. "So, I've been waiting to hear. Did Mr. Barnes find anything?" she asked.

"Yes!" Christopher held up a file.

"Unfortunately," Dana opened it up, "we looked through it, and there isn't anything different from what we already knew." She spread out some of the headlines on the table.

BEDFORD MAN ACCUSED OF ROBBING FROM CHURCH
BEDFORD ROBBERY SUSPECT PLEADS NOT GUILTY
CHURCH MEMBERS OUTRAGED OVER "LOST" MONEY
THOU SHALT NOT STEAL?

Charlotte felt a lump growing in her throat. "Oh my, these . . . . these are from newspapers all around Nebraska."

Christopher nodded. "Mr. Barnes said it was quite a story. He also said I still have a couple of weeks to work on *my* story. He wouldn't run it anyway until it was closer to the open house thing at church. He said he thought it might be a good advertisement for it—it will give people something to talk about."

"Oh, dear. This isn't how it was supposed to be at all. The church wants to have a celebration of the beginnings of the church. They want to display the highlights of our congregation over the years." Charlotte rose and moved toward the phone. "Maybe I should call Mr. Barnes and explain. Maybe I need to call Pastor Evans too and apologize. If anything happens to darken the mood of this celebration I won't forgive myself."

"Charlotte, wait." Dana rose from her chair and hurried to her side. "You don't need to do anything yet. Christopher is still working on the article. If Mr. Barnes does run it, it won't be for a couple of weeks. Why don't we just wait and see how everything plays out? Like I tell my kids at school, no need to make a drama of things."

Charlotte nodded. "I guess you're right. I'm pretty sure we're not going to find any more information about my granddaddy, but it gave us an interesting week."

"Don't give up yet, Grandma. Maybe we'll figure it out," Christopher said. "Dylan and I have plans to go to the library after school tomorrow. Mr. Barnes said a lady there has some old photographs and stuff."

"Oh, yes, Emily told me about that too. Maybe I'll meet you there. If anything, perhaps I can borrow some photos for the open house."

"That's the spirit!" Dana turned back to the table. "Oh, Christopher, don't forget to tell your grandma what else Mr. Barnes shared with you."

"There's more?" Charlotte joined them at the table.

"Well," Christopher explained, "while Mr. Barnes was researching he came across some other stuff. He doesn't know if it's connected to our mystery, but maybe." Christopher handed Charlotte a photocopy of another old newspaper article with the headline

STAGE ROBBED THREE TIMES IN TEN DAYS
PASSENGERS ON STAGE WHEN ROBBED
ROBBER LEAVES HAT BEHIND

"Hmm. That's a scintillating headline but Elijah made no mention of being robbed. It would have made everything a whole lot easier if he had been."

"That's true, but he could have been robbed without knowing it," Dana pointed out. "He was carrying the bag around; maybe someone who happened to be in town saw it and took it. Just because Elijah was friends with most people doesn't mean they were all trustworthy characters. If Bedford was anything like Omaha . . . well, he's lucky if he *wasn't* robbed!"

"Very true. I was just hoping for something more concrete from the news stories. I suppose if something was printed in 1879 that could have proved his innocence they would have figured it out then." Charlotte sighed.

"Don't worry, Grandma. We'll get to the bottom of the history mystery sooner or later," Christopher assured her before heading upstairs to do some homework.

Dana moved to the window and Charlotte saw a look of concern cross her face. "Is something bothering you, dear?" she asked.

Dana sighed. "I'm worried about the wedding. I hope the weather is going to be okay. It would be nice to be able to take some outside photos too."

"Oh, I love outside photos. Those always look so nice."

"Well, I don't know if it's going to happen. We don't even have a photographer yet. I brought these photographers' portfolios over for Pete to look at later. I've looked through them fifty times each, and I need Pete's opinion."

"Pete's opinion?"

Dana nodded. "I've narrowed it down to two, and I told Pete he could have the final choice."

"You're letting Pete have the final choice?" Charlotte reached for the first portfolio. Inside were photos of couples inside churches. She flipped through the pages. "Are you sure you want Pete picking out your photographer?" Charlotte chuckled.

"Yes, I've made so many decisions that I thought I should let him make a few. I don't want Pete to think the wedding is all about me."

Charlotte glanced up. "Actually, it *is* all about you!"

Dana looked at Charlotte. Her jaw dropped and then her eyes narrowed. "What? It's *our* wedding. It's not only about me."

Charlotte rose and hurried to Dana's side. "Oh, I didn't mean to make it sound bad. It's just that . . . think about it. If you left everything completely up to Pete, what do you think the wedding would be like?"

Dana pursed her lips. "We'd probably have it in the barn. He'd wear his jeans and his John Deere cap. Trudy the cow would be my maid of honor." Dana giggled. "And instead of throwing rice the guests could toss hay in the sky."

"Exactly."

"So are you saying that I'm not thinking about Pete—his likes—by planning the wedding with all the frou-frou stuff?"

"Not at all. I think Pete is happy about all of it, or at least nearly all of it."

"Yeah, he's complained quite a bit about having to wear a tux."

"But he's going to wear it. And he's going to enjoy the decorations and the frou-frou cake and all the flowers, not because it's his type of thing, but because he loves you and knows it will make you happy."

Tears filled Dana's eyes. "You know, I've never thought about that before. I—well, I was getting frustrated because he wasn't helping. Or he just kept telling me, 'Whatever you decide.' I thought he just wasn't interested." One tear broke through and slipped down Dana's cheek. "I almost thought he was having second thoughts about marrying me."

"Oh, honey." Charlotte pulled Dana into an embrace. "I'm so sorry. I didn't know you were feeling this way. Darling, you know Pete. He thinks *pretty* is a half-pound hamburger! And honestly, I truly think he'd rather have you make all the decisions. He wants *you* to be happy. He wants this to be a very special day—everything *you* dreamed of."

Dana pulled back, nodded, and then slid back into the chair. She took a deep breath.

Charlotte sat next to her and mindlessly stirred her coffee. "Just think of it this way, all little girls like to imagine their wedding day. They dream about it from the time they're little. I know I did. I remember being ten, lying in bed, and imagining my wedding day. And what do you think ten-year-old boys are lying there thinking about?"

"Hmm. Fishing, hunting, dirt bikes, skateboards. Or in Christopher's case, storms, tornadoes, his dog, and becoming the next star reporter." Dana pulled the second portfolio toward her. "Okay, then you can help me decide, and we can just show Pete when he gets here. Come to think of it, he'll probably be relieved."

"I think you're right."

Charlotte watched as they flipped through pages. "Looking at these, a sunny, spring day *would* be perfect for the wedding." She smiled. "Another thing to add to my growing prayer list."

IT HADN'T TAKEN MUCH to talk Dana into staying for dinner. Now, as the sun sank on the distant horizon, their bellies were full of spaghetti, and Dana didn't seem to be in a hurry to head out. It was nice, relaxing. Charlotte let out a contented sigh as she finished drying the last of the dinner dishes. After their talk about wedding plans, she had to admit she was starting to grow excited about the big day.

Pete chatted with Bob in the living room, and Dana sat at the dining room table, glancing over Emily's posters.

"Emily, I'm so impressed." Dana put on her teacher smile. "This project is great. Can you tell me about it?"

Emily shrugged. "Two of my friends and I are doing a project on the early settlers and the railroad. Most of them around Bedford bought land from the railroad, and . . ." She shrugged again. "We're just going to talk about how the towns sprouted up along the railroad line and how the people lived and stuff."

"I've read a little about that before. I think I remember the land being really cheap," Dana said.

"Three dollars an acre," Charlotte said. "I think that's what I read in my great-grandmother's journal."

"You have your great-grandmother's journal?" Dana asked.

"Haven't I shown you Lavina's diary?"

"No. I can't say you have. How wonderful! Where did you get it?"

For the next hour Dana, Charlotte, and Emily went through the diary pages once again. They teared up at some of Lavina's entries; others made them laugh.

"Wow, did you read this one about her family?" Dana asked.

"I might have but go ahead and read it again," Charlotte answered.

July 20, 1881

Today is my baby sister Amelia's birthday. I wrote her a letter last week, but I haven't been to town to post it yet. I wish I had a picture of Henry to include with it. I think that out of all my family Henry looks the most like Amelia. Maybe it's his eyes—as blue as the sky on a bright Nebraska day and sparkling slightly so that they always appear to be laughing.

I haven't seen Amelia in five years, since the day after my wedding when I joined Elijah on the train heading west. Of course "west" then was St. Louis. At the time I didn't believe we were going any farther than that. I couldn't have guessed then that I'd have a child my parents and sisters would never see.

Oh my, I do have a disagreeable disposition today, don't I?

Before—well, just before, Elijah and I had been planning a trip back home to see our families. He'd saved up a little bit from each paycheck. We had planned on being there for Independence Day, but it never happened.

For a while, even after all the problems started, I

thought we still had enough money to go. In the back of my mind I'd always thought that if things didn't work out here we could always just move back to Maryland and stay there for good. My hope was that we would make a fresh start and no one would know us—or the accusations that had been strapped to our backs.

I only found out later—at least six months later—that the go-back-home money was gone. Every penny of it. At first Elijah wouldn't tell me what he'd done with it. He said it was between him and God. Then I started to worry. Maybe he was a gambling man like some of the people from town said—although looking back now, that made no sense. When did he have time to gamble? That man was always working. And who would he gamble with? The sheep? The goats?

It was only later, during a weak moment, that Elijah confessed. He'd given all our savings to the church—every penny of it. He said it was only right after what had happened. He said it wasn't even a fraction of what was missing, but at least it made him feel better. I suppose for a moment his heart didn't ache quite as much.

I wish Amelia were here today. I'd tell her the story over a cup of tea. Mama too. What I would do to see Mama's gentle gaze, which always told me she cared.

Charlotte wiped her eyes, and as she glanced around she noticed that Dana was choked up too. Even Emily's eyes were glistening.

"Wow, that puts things in perspective. A few little wedding details don't seem like such a big deal."

"Oh, Dana." Charlotte pulled her into a close embrace. The pink sweater Dana wore was soft, and her hair smelled like apples. "I'm so glad you're joining our family. And you'll see. The wedding is going to be perfectly beautiful."

Dana pulled away slowly. "I guess I should head home. I need to rest up before facing all my classes tomorrow. Those high schoolers sure know how to drain the life out of you." Dana winked at Emily.

"Haha, very funny." Emily gave Dana a quick hug.

"Pete, time to go," Dana said as she went to the door and slipped her winter boots on.

"Aren't you bossy! You're acting like you rule the roost already. For the next month I'm still a bachelor."

Laughter filled the room, so loud and boisterous that it made Charlotte jump.

"Pete, give up that idea now." Bob laughed again. "If you want to make it to your first anniversary, that is."

Chapter Twenty-Three

Charlotte smiled as she walked up the steps of the library Wednesday afternoon, remembering the days when she used to bring her own kids here for story hour. That seemed like a lifetime ago, yet inside the library little had changed.

Charlotte entered the front door and looked behind the front desk. Her smile faded. Christopher and Dylan were sitting behind the counter on plastic chairs. Edna was checking out books for a mother with her toddler, and her eyes met Charlotte's gaze.

"There you go; enjoy these books. *The Very Hungry Caterpillar* is one of my favorites." Edna smiled at the woman, but Charlotte could tell she was anything but happy.

"There you are, Charlotte. I tried to call you at home three times, but Bob said you were already in town."

"I had to run some errands." She looked toward the boys, who stared at her with guilty faces. "Is there a problem?"

As Charlotte neared the counter, the scent of Edna's talcum powder met her nose.

"You should ask *them*."

"Boys, did you go behind the library counter? You know the rules."

"It was worse than that." Edna placed a fist on her hip. "They took the key and went into the new museum room without supervision. I was helping another patron, and they slipped in."

"We were just trying to look for clues for the mystery," Christopher said. "Miss June said she was going to meet us here and help us, but she didn't show up."

"June had to go visit a friend in the hospital. There are some places that are off limits to kids without supervision. And in addition to that, I found the dark-haired one using the copy machine reserved for library staff only."

"I'm so sorry, Edna. You're right. They shouldn't have disobeyed the rules. Boys, can you apologize?"

"We did." Dylan stood. "We said we were sorry."

"Okay, but please apologize again. I want to hear it."

"I'm sorry, Miss Edna." Christopher gave her his innocent face.

"I'm sorry, Miss Edna," Dylan echoed.

"Okay, boys. Get your things and get in the car."

Dylan and Christopher did so without hesitation.

Charlotte leaned forward on the counter. "I'm sorry about this. I will give them a talking-to on the drive home."

"You do that." Edna sighed. "And although their motives are good, I also don't want them wasting their time."

"What do you mean?"

"Well, Christopher told me he's working with you to prove your great-grandfather didn't steal that money."

"Yes, and you think it's a waste of time?"

"I've talked to a lot of people. I've read almost every book about the history of the area. The loss of the money is something I am familiar with, and pretty much no one has been able to discover any other answer for where the money went."

Charlotte brushed her hair behind her ear and cocked her head. "Are you saying you believe my great-grandpa was guilty?"

"Oh, honey, I hope you don't feel that what I think about that incident is any reflection on how I feel about you. No matter what anyone says, one bad apple does not spoil the whole bunch."

Charlotte nodded, but she didn't know what to say or how to respond. Everyone had the right to an opinion, she supposed.

"Thank you. Like I said, I'll talk to the boys."

"Good enough, and don't let yourself worry about that old money anymore. What's past is past. Oh, yes, and here are the copies for the girls' project. Lily's dad has already come in and paid for them."

Charlotte took the photos and nodded, but as she walked out to the car she didn't know if she agreed with Edna's comment. "What's past is past," she had said. *Does this matter, God? Should it?* She thought about God's Word and how His story continued through the generations, through good times and bad. Many times throughout the Bible, God said, "I am the God of Abraham, Isaac, and Jacob."

She got into the car, and the boys remained silent. Her

mind continued to wander as she headed toward Dylan's house.

"I am the God of Elijah, Albert, William, and Charlotte," she whispered. "Of Denise, of Christopher . . ."

"What are you saying, Grandma?" Christopher asked.

"Oh, I was just mumbling to myself, wondering if we should give up."

"I don't think so, Grandma." Christopher patted his backpack. "I wrote down something I think might help."

"Some new information to keep us going?"

"Oh, *I* think so." Dylan's voice piped up from the backseat. "Just wait until you hear what Christopher figured out. Christopher, do you have those copies?"

Charlotte could hear Christopher unzipping his backpack and rummaging through the items. Then she felt a tap on her shoulder.

"Here, Grandma, do you want to look? It's really cool."

"Not while I'm driving. When we get home, okay?"

"Do you promise?" Christopher's voice noted urgency.

"Yes, of course. I'll look at them at home."

"You're gonna like it," Dylan said. "Really, really like it."

"THANKS FOR GIVING US a ride home, Sam." Emily pulled out the peanut better and jelly and started to make sandwiches for a snack. "Do you want one sandwich or two, Andrea?" she asked.

"Two, please," Andrea piped up. "And, yes, thank you, Sam." Then she turned to Emily. "Can I get started on the poster?"

"Yeah, sure." Emily shrugged.

Sam pulled off his boots and unzipped his coat.

"You're welcome. Maybe it will help me get back in Grandma's good graces."

"Yeah, she seems a little freaked out by Kendall."

"That's because she doesn't even know her. She hasn't even given her a chance."

"Do you blame her? Some mysterious girl pops up out of nowhere, and you're traipsing all over town with her."

"Man, Em, you totally sound like an old woman. Are you Grandma's clone or something?"

"No, but what do you expect? You haven't given Grandma a choice."

Sam focused his eyes on Emily's. "What are you saying?"

Emily shrugged. "I'm just saying that it would be cool if you brought Kendall around some time. If she's *really* nice, then that shouldn't be a problem."

"Yeah, well, I don't know if I want to do that."

"Why?"

"Because it might turn out Grandma will start liking Kendall, and then she'll be sad when I stop hanging around with her."

"You're going to stop?"

Sam shrugged. "I'm not sure. I might. She's really cool, and she reminds me of . . ." Sam paused.

"Mom?"

Sam's eyes widened. "Do you think so too?"

"Yeah, she laughs like Mom. The first time I heard Kendall laugh at school my heart totally started pounding. Maybe they walk the same too. I don't know, but I agree that Kendall reminds me of Mom. What I don't understand is why you'd stop talking to her."

"It's complicated. There's stuff you don't need to know. I have some questions, some things I need to find answers for." Sam zipped his jacket back up and pulled on his boots. "Anyway, I'm heading out."

"Where?"

Sam grabbed a scarf and wrapped it around his neck. "I'm just going to see what Kendall is up to tonight."

"Wouldn't it be easier just to call?"

"Of course, but then it would be easier for her to say she's busy too. See you in a little bit."

Emily rolled her eyes as her brother headed out the door. Then she took the two paper plates with peanut butter and jelly sandwiches to Andrea. "Here you go. I'll pour us some milk too."

"Great, thanks." Andrea smiled. "So what do we have left to do?" she asked as she took a big bite of her sandwich.

"We have everything we need. We just have to figure out who's going to say what in our report."

"I can talk about the Czech newspaper ads, and the different settlers from all over the world," Andrea volunteered.

"Okay, I'll talk about the railroad and how Nebraska towns popped up because of the depots."

"Yeah, and how some of the depots got there because the steam engines needed water towers where they could fill up."

"What should we have Lily talk about?" Emily tapped her pencil against the table.

"She can hold the signs and operate the train." Andrea laughed.

The door opened, and Grandma entered. Christopher followed, carrying a large box.

"The train!" Emily jumped up. "Thanks, Grandma, for picking it up for me. Did you tell Miss Middleton hi for me?"

"Yes, I did. Sadly, she didn't look very well."

"That's not good. I wonder if I can do something for her when she gets back from visiting her niece."

"Emily, that is a wonderful and very thoughtful idea. Her house could use a good going over; that's for sure." Grandma turned to put her purse away.

Emily knelt on the floor and looked at the photo on the side of the box. She smiled as she imagined how the class would respond. "No one will have a presentation like this."

Andrea approached and squatted down to take a look. "We might even be able to keep up with Ashley's cooking presentation." Andrea returned to the table and opened her notebook. "Or at least we'll be second best..."

Grandma took off her jacket and hung it on the back of the dining room chair. She rubbed the back of her neck, and Emily thought she looked tired. "Okay, Christopher. You better head out to the barn and do your chores."

"Grandma, now?" Christopher looked stricken. "Don't you want to find out what I discovered at the library?"

"After dinner there will be plenty of time. The animals are waiting. Grandpa is waiting too, and I don't think he's going to be happy if he does all the chores by himself."

"Can I go with you to see the animals?" Andrea jumped from her seat. As she did, her arm hit her glass of milk. It tipped over, spilling.

"The posters!" Emily rushed to the table, scooping them up. Thankfully the milk spilled in the opposite direction, making the paper plates soggy. Emily hurried to the kitchen for a towel to clean up the mess.

"Oh, no! I'm so sorry." Andrea followed Emily into the kitchen, grabbing another towel. "I've made such a mess."

Grandma hurried to help. She took the paper plates and tossed them in the trash. "No use making a fuss. It's only milk."

Emily wiped up the milk, and then picked up her grandma's coat. Milk had dripped down the front of it. "Do you want me to throw it in the washer?"

"Yes, let me get my keys out first." Grandma stuck her hand into the pocket. She pulled out her keys and some envelopes.

"Oh, no! I forgot these were in here. I hope they didn't get wet." She placed the envelopes on the kitchen counter.

Emily eyed them. "What are these? They look really old."

"Miss Middleton gave them to me. She thought I might be able to get information from them. The only problem is that they're written in German. I'm hoping Greta Harbinger will be able to help me read them, but I haven't gotten ahold of her yet."

Emily turned to Andrea. "Do you know German?"

Andrea shrugged. "A little bit. I only took two years."

"Two years?" Emily poked her arm. "You know lots of languages. It's unbelievable."

Christopher just shook his head and headed out to do his chores.

Andrea opened the first letter and her eyes widened. "This letter . . . it's not German. It's Czech!"

"Czech?"

"Yes, my language." Andrea laughed. "The words are a little faded in spots, but I think I can read it."

"Really? Grandma, did you hear that?"

"I sure did." Grandma hurried to the desk and grabbed her notebook. "Do you think you could tell us what they say? At least the first one. We can read the rest of them after dinner."

"Okay. You can start cooking and I'll read this. It might take a minute for me to figure it out."

Andrea sat down on the living room couch. She held the letter close to her face and narrowed her gaze, concentrating.

Finally, after ten minutes, she sat up straight. "Okay, I think I can read this now."

Emily sat by her side and looked at the words on the paper. Then she waited as Andrea read: "It's to Iva Spilko. *'Dear Sister, I hope this letter finds you better than it finds us. We just had our first prairie fire. It is something we hope to . . .'*"

Andrea lifted her head. "I think this says *never*, but it's hard to read." She resumed her reading. "*'It is something we hope to never see again. We lost it all. We lost our mule and the old heifer that we had picketed nearby.*

"*I was thinking yesterday and I had an idea of where the lost bag could be. You said you saw Elijah Coleman with the bag on his way to the church. You also wrote that when you found Mr. Coleman at the church site he was asleep propped up next to the foundation of the church but there was no bag to be found. Do you think someone could have taken the bag while he slept? Perhaps the men who came to do construction saw someone?'*"

Emily looked toward her grandma, and they locked eyes. "It's more than I've ever heard before. Iva actually saw my granddaddy when he was on his way to the church and then after he got there! I suppose we can narrow the loss down to that area."

Emily had never seen her grandma so excited.

"Andrea, do you think you can read the next letter too?"

"Grandma, do you want me to make dinner? You know, while you go over the letters with Andrea?"

"You'd do that?"

"Sure, if everyone else doesn't mind vegetarian lasagna." Emily hurried into the kitchen. "I think I've got everything I'll need."

"I hope you don't mind," Emily heard her grandma saying to Andrea. "I thought they were in German. I never expected this."

SAM PARKED IN FRONT of the small travel trailer. It was one of the few in the RV park. In the summer this park was full, especially around fair days. But this time of year only a few spots were filled.

A large truck was parked next to Hank's smaller one. It was one Sam didn't recognize. He hoped he wasn't catching Hank and Kendall at a bad time. He thought about getting back in the car and heading home, but the trailer door swung open.

Kendall stood there in sweats and a T-shirt. "Sam, hurry! All the cold air is coming in. I heard your car pull up." She rubbed her arms and shifted her weight from side to side.

Sam hurried inside. It was small, and every surface was covered with stuff—or what his grandpa would call junk. Hank sat on an upholstered bench that looked like it converted into a bed. Another man sat beside him, and they were looking over the items Hank, Kendall, and Sam had found on their recent treasure hunt, including the comb and spoon that Sam had taken home to show his family.

"Hey, Sam. You're just in time. I was just showing Mr. Driggers what we found."

"Mr. Driggers? Like at the farm?"

"Yes, of course. I wanted to show him the things I found before I posted them for sale—just to make sure there wasn't something sentimental he wanted to keep. It was his wife's great-grandparents' soddie, you know."

Sam scratched his head. "So, wait. Mr. Driggers, you know about it?"

Mr. Driggers nodded. "Yes, of course. I wish I could have been there but I had to be up in Harding."

Sam turned to Hank again. "But I don't understand. You said you hoped people didn't see us. You wanted me to keep it a secret."

Kendall laughed. "Sam, did you think we *snuck* onto people's property and stole their stuff?" She placed a hand on her hip. "Seriously?"

Sam felt heat rising to his cheeks. "Don't look at me that way. I didn't know."

"I guess you wouldn't have known, would you?" Hank laughed. "Maybe I should have made that clear up front. I'm sorry if it seemed like we weren't on the up and up."

"Yeah, okay, but what I still don't understand is why it has to be a secret. If the farmer knows, then what's the problem?" Sam lifted a silver spoon from the tray and fingered it. It was the one he'd given back to Kendall.

"The problem isn't the farmer—it's the other untrained treasure hunters," Hank said. "They *do* sneak onto the land without permission. They don't know how to search right, and they make a mess of things. When word gets out that antiques are found at old home sites, everyone and his brother gets into the act. Besides the destruction of property, valuable items disappear, never to be found again."

Sam smiled and then sat down next to Hank. "So my guess is that the farmer gets a percentage of the money you make?"

"Of course. It's only fair."

"We work together." Kendall placed a hand on Sam's shoulder. "We share the work, share the treasure, and share the profit." Then she dropped her hand and looked away. "Then, after we work our way through an area, we move on. It's as it's always been."

"Modern-day explorers. That's what I call us," Hank said confidently.

Kendall didn't look quite as confident.

He felt bad for her. Not only about the way she and her father were viewed, even by her father himself, but also because as soon as she made friends somewhere, no doubt it would soon be time to move on.

Sam put his hand on Kendall's back and leaned close to her ear. "Sorry I ever doubted you," he said.

CHARLOTTE FELT WARM all over, and at the moment it didn't matter that she was completely turning over dinner duties to Emily. Or that Andrea and Emily were actually supposed to be doing homework instead of cooking dinner and translating letters for her.

Andrea opened the next letter and began again.

> "Sorry I didn't write yesterday. I was out in the fields with Abraham putting out the corn and sorghum seed. We are hoping these crops will help with our losses. Quite a number of farm animals in the area were lost in the fire. We are thankful that there was no loss of human life. The farm south of us lost the new framed house. Thankfully all their sheep were saved. They have five hundred head. They saved them by taking them into the plowed field where the fire couldn't burn.
>
> I talked to Abraham about the problems with your church."

Andrea lifted her head again. "It says something else here, but it's right on the fold of the paper. I can't read it."

Charlotte didn't realize she'd been holding her breath. "Oh, it's okay. You can just skip that part."

"Okay." Andrea narrowed her gaze and looked at the page again. The door opened, and Bob and Christopher entered.

"Lookie here. It's a little Miss Betty Crocker," Bob called. "Do you need help setting the table, Emily?"

"Sure, Grandpa. Thanks."

"Christopher, can you do that?" Bob chuckled.

"But Grandpa! I want to show Grandma what I found in the library."

"After dinner, I promise," Charlotte said. "This is important."

She offered Christopher a smile. She could hear him banging around the kitchen, pulling out the dishes.

Charlotte turned back to Andrea. "Okay. Go on."

"Sister, it's very hard for me to ask this, but do you have any money that we can borrow? Thirty to forty dollars would be enough. Our neighbor who lost their house is leaving. They are talking about Minnesota. We have a chance to buy their heifer, since ours was lost. After the fire, no one is able to buy on credit. I used to be able to get groceries on 30 days time but the owner of the general store lost property too."

Andrea looked up. "It goes on, but it's just news of deaths and births and stuff."

When the door opened again, Charlotte expected to see Pete, but instead it was Sam, followed by Kendall.

"Well, Sam. You brought a guest." She stood, approached Kendall, and stretched out her hand, noticing that the girl wore a sweater large enough to fit Bob. It hung nearly to her knees. Yet the drabness of the sweater was brightened by Kendall's rainbow scarf and bright purple stocking cap.

"I'm Charlotte, Sam's grandma."

Kendall took her hand. "Hey, I'm Kendall. I hope this isn't an imposition. Sam said it would be fine."

"Not an imposition at all." Charlotte tried to switch gears from the news in the letters about Elijah's nap and the construction workers at the church to their additional guest for dinner.

Charlotte looked to Emily. "Do you, uh, need help?"

"I'm making a big lasagna, see?" Emily held up Charlotte's

largest pan, now lined with lasagna noodles. Then Charlotte watched as Emily quickly added a layer of ricotta cheese mixture and a layer of spinach, followed by a layer of jarred pasta sauce. Then she repeated it.

"I suppose I could make a salad." Charlotte moved to the fridge, taking out the lettuce, carrots, and tomatoes she'd picked up earlier that day.

"I can help." Kendall moved to the sink, pushed up the sleeves on her sweater, and washed her hands.

"Oh, that's really not necessary. I think we'll be fine." Charlotte looked into the girl's face, and she discovered that hidden under all those layers of clothes was a pretty girl with green eyes and a kind smile.

"Really, I don't mind at all." Kendall grabbed a salad bowl from the drying rack on the counter and then placed it next to the cutting board. "It's just me and my dad at home. I'm used to doing all the cooking." She laughed.

Charlotte liked her laugh.

"Just making a salad is getting off easy, believe me," Kendall said.

"Okay, fine. I suppose if you don't mind..." Charlotte glanced at Sam, who was leaning against the wall with a smile across his face, obviously enjoying the interaction.

Charlotte's stomach churned. *He set me up. He knew I'd have to be kind to the girl, to give her a chance.* With those thoughts came a realization of how things must have looked to Sam. Here she'd been attempting to prove her granddaddy's innocence despite the accusations against him.

"Sam," she said, meeting his gaze, "can you help Andrea clear all the project stuff off the table and then help

Christopher set it? And put on the good dishes; we have guests."

Sam's grin widened. "Sure, Grandma. I'd love to."

Kendall dried her hands on the dishtowel and then reached for Charlotte's arm. Her voice was gentle. "Mrs. Stevenson, do you have a minute?"

"Of course." Charlotte paused, looking into the girl's face.

"I just wanted to apologize. In fact, I asked Sam if he could invite me over so I could. He didn't think today was the best day for me to come, but I insisted."

"No, Kendall, it's okay, really. It's fine. Things are a little busy, but they always are around here."

"Okay, good." Kendall looked away and then met Charlotte's eyes again. "I asked Sam to keep something a secret. I realize now I shouldn't have. I'm sure it made it seem like we were up to no good, and I shouldn't have put Sam in that position." Kendall paused, and then she nodded, as if urging herself on.

"You see, my father and I work with farmers to find antiques left by settlers on their land. We don't like many people to know about it because if word gets out, everyone becomes a treasure hunter. But I just wanted you to know that what we're doing is done under an agreement with the farmers. I'm sorry I didn't trust you. I can see now you have a lovely family and that you would have kept our secret."

"Oh, Kendall." Charlotte felt a rush of guilt wash over her—guilt mixed with relief. "I have to admit I'm happy to hear that what you're doing is legal." Charlotte nervously chuckled. "But, dear girl, I'm the one who needs to apologize. I was the one who listened to unfounded rumors and assumed the worst. Why don't we start over from here? It can be a fresh start."

Kendall nodded. Then she stepped back and extended a hand that was half hidden under a long sleeve. Charlotte reached out and accepted it.

"Hello, Mrs. Stevenson. My name is Kendall Richardson."

"Hello, Kendall," Charlotte said. "Nice to meet you. And I mean that. I really, really do."

CHARLOTTE TOOK THE last bite of her lasagna and noticed Christopher fidgeting in his seat. During the meal she'd enjoyed listening to Andrea and Kendall telling stories of the places they had lived, and more than once she'd had to scold Christopher for trying to interrupt.

Then, just as Andrea was finishing telling about last year's school trip to Italy, a spout of words burst from Christopher's lips.

"Grandma, can I please share what Dylan and I found at the library? I promise it will *only* take five minutes."

"You're right. I'm so sorry. I've been putting it off all evening. What did you want to show me?"

"Finally!" Christopher jumped from his seat and hurried to his backpack by the door. He pulled out two copies of something and brought them to her.

Charlotte looked at the photos. Emily rose from her seat and came around to get a better look too.

One was a photo of a woman and a little girl. Emily pointed to it.

"Oh, yeah, I saw that one, although it was big and framed. How did you get a copy?"

"Dylan was looking through a box, and he found it. The date said July 4, 1879."

"Do you think they're the ones who stole the money?" Sam leaned over to get a better look too. "Hmm, she sure does look like a robber."

"No, don't look at the lady." Christopher shook his head. "Look behind her. Look at the building."

Charlotte lifted the paper closer to her face. Because it was a photocopy of an old, black-and-white picture, it was hard to distinguish what it was. "Are you sure that's a building? It looks like a stage or maybe a blanket on the ground."

"No, I see that too, Grandma. It's a floor or something, like a foundation," Emily said. "June—the lady who's working at the library—said it was the basement for Bedford Community Church."

"Really? That's interesting. It makes sense since the letter Andrea just translated for us said that construction workers had been at the church the day the bag disappeared."

"Okay, now look at the other one." Christopher pointed to the second photocopy. The picture had been taken at the same angle, and the wooden platform was only half done.

"I don't understand."

Christopher grinned. "The date on the photo said March 31, 1879. Which means . . ."

"Which means it was taken the day before the money disappeared. They were working on building the foundation!" Charlotte placed her fingers over her lips.

"Is it possible that Elijah could have put the bag inside the footings and didn't remember doing that?" Bob asked.

"Remember? That one letter said he fell asleep," Andrea said.

"Yes, Lavina's journal did too. It mentioned Elijah resting." Charlotte scanned the excited faces around her. "And if he was disoriented when he woke up, and he just went on home—why, the foundation could have been finished when he went to the safe the next day. Even if he retraced his steps, he wouldn't have found the bag."

"If so, I know how we can find it." It was Kendall's voice.

"Oh, yeah!" Sam jumped from his chair. "Grandma, do you still have the key to the church? I know how we can totally find out tonight."

Chapter Twenty-Four

Charlotte had tried Pastor Evans one more time on Emily's cell phone. Finally, after three rings, he'd picked up and had agreed to meet them at the church. Now she looked around at the faces of those assembled with her in the church basement: Pastor Evans, Bob, Emily, Andrea, Christopher, Sam, Kendall.

She turned to Bob. "I don't know. What do you think? Should we go ahead and try?"

Bob tucked his hands into his jacket pockets. "I don't see how it will hurt anything." He turned to the preacher standing beside him.

Pastor Evans looked at Kendall. "Start her up. Let's get this thing rolling."

"Okay, sure. Just as long as I have your permission." She glanced at Sam. "After all, this *is* private property." She winked.

"It's also community property," Bob added. "It's our church. And this is something I bet the community will be very interested in."

Kendall slipped her arm into a loop and grabbed the handle of the metal detector, and then Charlotte watched as she pushed some buttons beside a small screen.

"That thing is cool." Christopher's eyes widened. "What are you doing?"

"I'm programming this to look for coins. See, on this screen there's a menu that allows you to pick out what you're looking for. It makes it more accurate."

"I had no idea those things were so complicated." Pastor Evans scratched his head.

"It's like it has a little computer," Charlotte observed.

"Well, most of them don't. This one is a little fancier. I've been begging for this model. I told my dad if he got it for me he wouldn't have to buy me another Christmas or birthday gift for five years."

Kendall flipped through the menu until she got to COINS. "Okay, it's set. It will be ready to go as soon as I turn it on. Where should I start?"

Charlotte looked around the basement, eyeing the well-worn wooden floor. Thanks to the efforts of the women's group, it was mostly clean.

"I think we should start in the corners," Emily suggested. "In the photo it showed that lady standing by one of the corners."

"Yes, but it's hard to tell which way she was facing since the only thing behind the church's foundation was prairie."

"I'll just pick one." Kendall moved to the north corner, and everyone followed. Then she flipped the machine on. It made a low buzzing sound. Slowly, she swept the round head of the machine over the area, back and forth.

"Folks." Sam spread his hands out. "Please give her room."

Everyone backed up, but only slightly.

As the metal detector moved along, Charlotte heard the smallest of beeps. Bob must have heard it too because he looked at her. "Do you hear that?"

"Actually, those are just the nails in the wooden foundation. If we find coins you'll hear a much louder beep."

Kendall continued on, covering the entire corner. Then she slowly moved along the wall.

Charlotte leaned closer to Sam. "She sure seems to know what she's doing."

Sam patted her back. "You haven't seen anything yet, Grandma. You should see her in the field."

"Can you go faster?" Andrea asked. "I cannot wait."

"Actually, I need to move the search head slowly. Otherwise we could miss something important."

"Is it going to do something—you know, to tell you if there's something there?" Emily asked.

"Yeah, when you pass over a target object there will be an audible signal," Kendall explained. "And fancier detectors, like this one, will even tell you how deep the object is."

Slowly, surely, she moved to the second corner. Then, just as she was about to move down the next wall there was a louder beep.

"I'm gonna push the locator button to narrow it in."

Beep, beep. The sounds were quiet. *Beep, beep, beep.* They got louder. Kendall moved the detector in the other direction. Again the beeps were quiet at first, and then they got louder.

It got louder still, and Sam put his finger on the spot on

the floor. Kendall moved the detector again. "Umm, a little to the right, see? That's where it's loudest."

Kendall looked at Bob. "Do you have that ax? I'm pretty sure there's a coin under there."

Bob stepped forward and Kendall stepped back.

"Are you sure, pastor?" Bob asked one more time.

Pastor Evans nodded. "Let her rip."

Bob looked behind him to make sure no one was there. Then he swung. The wood split in a terrific crack. He did the same thing ten more times until he'd cut out a hole about eight inches in diameter. Then Bob knelt to the ground.

"Here's the flashlight." Christopher stepped forward. Bob took it from him and clicked it on. Then he pointed it down into the hole. "I think I see something. Emily, come here and hold this flashlight for me."

Emily did as she was told, and Bob reached his hand down.

"Bob, are you sure? There could be spiders or something." Charlotte sighed.

"Too late now, Grandma," Christopher mumbled.

Bob's hand reemerged. Then he stood and opened his hand. In it was a silver coin.

"Wow! We found something." Andrea bounced where she was.

"Yes, but it's only one. Do you see more?" Christopher took the flashlight back and peered down the hole.

Bob stared into the hole again too. "No, I didn't see any more. Do you?"

Christopher sighed. "No, nothing. Just dirt and stuff."

Bob handed the coin to Charlotte, and she held it up to the light. On the front was a woman in a dress with a shield that said LIBERTY. "Eighteen seventy," Charlotte read.

Kendall moved next to her. "That's a really old and valuable coin. Ones in good condition like this one go for a couple thousand dollars."

"No way! Are you serious?" Emily's jaw dropped open.

Although it was a great find, Charlotte felt the hope puffed up inside her deflate. "It could have just fallen from someone's pocket. Just because we found it doesn't mean there are more."

"Well, we can keep looking; maybe there's more somewhere else."

Kendall turned on the metal detector again. She had hardly gone ten feet when the beeping started again. This time it was louder, stronger. She swept the detector back and forth, but the sound didn't fade.

"Sounds like you found another coin!" Christopher called.

"Make that *coins*." Sam reached his hand toward the ax. "I'd be happy to do this one, Grandpa."

Everyone stepped back again, and in six strikes a large gap was in the floor.

"Here's the flashlight, Sam." Christopher held it out.

Sam pointed to Charlotte. "Give it to Grandma. I think she needs to be the one to look."

Christopher did as he was told. With shaking hands, Charlotte took the flashlight from him. There wasn't a sound in the room as she knelt on the floor. She was almost afraid to look.

Then, taking in a deep breath, she pointed the flashlight into the hole. Easily visible, not a foot away, was a bag. It was dusty, but the words were still clear: UNITED STATES MAIL.

IT TOOK ALL THE SELF-CONTROL they possessed, but they waited to open the bag until Pete and Dana met them at the church.

Inside were several silver dollars—just like the first one they'd found. They also found a stack of paper bank notes of varying denominations.

Also inside was a stack of letters. "Oh, look. Here's one from Wilma to her sister Peggy—the one Peggy confirmed had never showed up."

"Now we know why," Sam quipped.

There were other letters too. Charlotte wanted more than anything to open them and read them, but she wouldn't. They all agreed the best thing to do would be to let them be handled by the postal authorities.

"Look, Charlotte." Dana touched her arm. "It's a letter from Lavina to someone back east."

"Yes, I'm not sure if it was a sister or a friend, but I'd recognize that handwriting anywhere."

"Well, Mom, you did it. You did it for Granddaddy." Pete wrapped an arm around Charlotte's shoulders.

"No, Pete, *we* did it. And we did it for *us*. For our family—past and future."

Chapter Twenty-Five

Nearly a week had passed since they'd found the bag, and it indeed had become the talk of the town. It also had become the talk of the church—important enough that the church leaders called a special board meeting.

"I wonder what they want to talk to us about?" Charlotte mused, playing with the zipper of her jacket as they waited, moving it up and then back down again.

Charlotte, Bob, Pete, Dana, and the kids sat in folding chairs along the hall just outside the church's meeting room.

"Even weirder that they wanted all of us to be here."

"Maybe they're going to give us the money we found and then we'll be able to buy dirt bikes to ride around the farm," Christopher said.

Pete squeezed the back of Christopher's neck. "I don't think so."

The door opened, and Pastor Evans motioned them inside. "Come in, folks, and bring your chairs. We don't have much room, and strong, hot coffee is all we have to offer, but I think this will be worth it."

As soon as they had carried their chairs into the room and were situated, Hannah's husband, Frank, stood.

He cleared his throat and began speaking while Bob reached over and took Charlotte's hand.

"On behalf of Bedford Community Church, we would like to offer you this document officially clearing Elijah Coleman's name of any wrongdoing." Frank moved across the room to Charlotte and handed her a piece of paper rolled up as a scroll with a red ribbon tied around it.

"Thank you," Charlotte managed to squeak out, pressing the document to her chest.

Nancy Evans rose, her smile spreading over her face like butter over hot corn. "We have something else. We want you to know that the postal authorities agreed to let us donate the letters and papers in the satchel to the Adams County Historical Society and their new museum room at the library. In addition, with Edna's help, copies of the letters will be given to any family members we can find, many of whom still live in Bedford."

"That's wonderful. Such a treasure," Charlotte heard Dana comment.

"We've also had some help figuring out what to do with the money." She motioned to a man sitting next to Pastor Evans, a man Charlotte didn't recognize. "This is Hank Richardson, Kendall's father. He put us in contact with a museum in Boston that's interested in the money. We're going to sell it for its historical worth and put the proceeds into the church's building-and-reconstruction fund, since that was its original purpose."

Mr. Richardson rose. "It was an honor to help represent

you folks. My daughter, Kendall, has said wonderful things about your family, Mr. and Mrs. Stevenson, and I appreciate your welcoming her into your home. I've been searching for treasure most of my life, but this discovery—and the people I've met here—well, they've made me decide that maybe some of the best treasures around are found in the company we keep. Thank you."

A few minutes later the meeting broke up, and the room erupted into several conversations, all going on at once. Hannah and Frank approached and offered quick hugs, but Charlotte wasn't focused on them. In the corner of the room, she saw Mr. Richardson slipping out.

"Excuse me, Hannah. I'll be right back."

"Mr. Richardson, it's so nice to meet you," Charlotte called, following him.

He turned and smiled, removing his cap and holding it in his hands. "Hank. You can call me Hank. Everyone does."

"Okay, Hank. I just wanted to say that I really appreciate your help—both with lending us your daughter's talents and with helping the church know what to do with the money."

He shrugged. "It's nothing. It's stuff like this that I live for. Makes it all worthwhile."

"Yes, well, I not only wanted to thank you, but I also think it would be great to have you and Kendall over for dinner sometime. I'm sure you have some fun stories to share."

Hank's face brightened. "Sounds good. Thank you. I'd better go now." He glanced at his watch. "I'm supposed to meet Kendall over at the dump. I have a feeling in my bones that it's going to be a day of discovery."

He walked away with a wave, and Charlotte crossed her arms and watched him go, enjoying the quiet of the hallway and the deep peace she felt inside before returning to the board room.

"I've been feeling that way, too," she whispered to herself. "Day of discovery. I like that."

Chapter Twenty-Six

"Are you nervous?" Charlotte asked Emily as they drove to the church for the open house. It was hard to believe how much had happened since they found the coins and cleared Granddaddy's name. Every morning she woke up excited about what they'd done.

"Nah, we've already done it in class and got an A. I don't think anyone from the church is going to grade us. Besides, I know everyone there. There shouldn't be any surprises."

The car drove up the small hill, and Bedford Community Church came into view. Charlotte's hand reached for the dashboard as if that would somehow lessen the surprise of the sea of cars that filled the parking lot. Cars even overflowed along the side of the highway.

"No surprises?" Bob chuckled. "Think again."

"Oh great, the whole town showed up." Emily looked down at her clothes. "I should have dressed better."

"Don't worry, sweetheart." Charlotte glanced back at Emily. "You look beautiful, and you will be *wonderful*."

Bob dropped everyone off in the church parking lot and drove away to find a place to park. As they started walking toward the building, Charlotte glanced at Sam. Ever since the other night, she'd wanted to talk to him. She thought about the day and everything it held. Charlotte knew if she didn't do it now she wouldn't have a chance to.

"Sam, can you hold up a minute?" she said.

Sam paused. The other kids did too.

"The rest of you go ahead. I need to talk to Sam just a minute."

The others walked on ahead, and Charlotte looked up into Sam's face. "Honey, I just want to apologize. I haven't been very fair to you or to Kendall. I jumped to all types of conclusions without really getting to know her. It wasn't fair to her or to you."

Sam's eyes were fixed on hers, and he nodded. "Thanks." He gave her a quick hug.

"No, wait, there's more." She hurried on before she changed her mind. "I still have a couple of questions that haven't been answered, like why she misses so much school and why you were out driving with her during school time."

"All right, Grandma. Just so you don't freak out again, I'll tell you," Sam said. "The day you saw us in her car we were out during an early lunch break—we have off-campus privileges, you know. And Kendall isn't in school full-time because she takes online college courses. She's actually really smart."

A huge wave of relief settled over Charlotte. She really liked Kendall and had hoped that there would be reasonable explanations to her questions.

"In that case, I'd like to see her around more often. And if you want to date—"

"Date? I just broke up with Arielle not too long ago. I don't think I'm ready to date."

"You're not?"

"No." Sam shook his head. "Just because I like hanging around with Kendall doesn't mean I want to date her. Or marry her. Or move along with her and her dad as they head out on their treasure-seeking adventures."

Charlotte patted his arm and turned to walk toward the church. "Well, that's good. I guess I was just jumping to a lot of conclusions. You'd think after all these years I'd stop getting carried away. Sometimes I wish this grandma thing were easier."

"Yeah, well, sometimes I wish this 'growing up and making your place in the world' thing were easier too. It seems like God should just hand me a map, and then all I'd have to do is follow it."

Charlotte waved to friends entering the building and then touched her grandson's arm, slowing the pace.

"Sam, this is a little of what I've been dealing with lately."

"What do you mean? You're not planning to move away and start a new life, are you, Grandma?" Sam chuckled.

"No, although some days I'm tempted to consider it." Charlotte smiled. "What I'm talking about is this little mystery I've been trying to solve. At first it was just something that piqued my interest. But then, as I realized it would continue to impact our family—and our family name—I became passionate about it. It became important for me to understand, to know the truth."

"Yeah, I'll say you were a little passionate about it. Those jeans I threw in the laundry room last week still aren't washed, and you've been quick to turn over the kitchen to anyone who's breathing."

"Well, not quite. But I see your point."

Sam pointed down to his dirty jeans, and Charlotte cringed.

"Okay, I'll wash them tomorrow, but what I wanted to tell you is that when this whole thing began I didn't know where to start. So I started with what I knew. The first thing I knew was that the money disappeared in my granddaddy's possession. It wasn't clear if it was lost or stolen. And then I kept looking for clues. They came from unexpected places. Some I hunted down, and others—like those Czech letters—were just placed in my path like unexpected gifts. Then, believe it or not, it was Christopher who figured out the most important part—figured out they happened to be building the foundation when the money disappeared. An unexpected Sherlock Holmes, don't you think?"

"Do you think that's what I need to do? Look for clues in my life? And pay attention to wisdom from unexpected people?"

"Yes, and also take time to listen to yourself, your heart. What excites you? What do you feel passionate about? Where do the clues point?"

Sam ran his fingers through his hair, brushing it back from his face like he always did when he was deep in thought. "Grandma, are you saying that God lays out our life's purpose in clues, and it's our job to figure it out?"

"Not exactly. I don't think he tries to trick us or make things difficult. Instead, I believe that as we move forward in the path already cleared, God shows us the next steps ahead."

"I suppose that makes sense. I'll have to think about that."

"And pray about it." Charlotte tucked her arm into his, and they strode together toward the church.

"Sure, Grandma," Sam agreed awkwardly.

They walked for a half minute longer.

"It's kind of crazy weird, you know."

Charlotte glanced up at him. "What is?"

"We've just done something good here. Something really good. That's *crazy weird*."

Pastor Evans was standing inside the church door. "Charlotte, Sam, it's great to see you."

"Good to see you too, pastor." Sam shook his hand.

Sam had turned to find a seat when the pastor's voice halted his steps.

"But, Sam, there is one thing that still needs to be fixed. It's that hole in the basement. I've been telling everyone it only took six swings to make that hole. You've got some arm there."

"Yes sir." Sam grinned. "Maybe my grandpa, Uncle Pete, and I will be here in the morning to fix it."

"Thank you, Sam." Pastor Evans winked. "Appreciate it."

TWENTY MINUTES LATER, Charlotte stared in awe at the crowd filling the fellowship hall to capacity at the church's open house. Emily, Lily, and Andrea were putting the finishing touches to their presentation at the front of the room. Christopher was putting the train together on the square table he and Bob had brought out from one of the Sunday school rooms.

Sam and Kendall were there too, posing for Rick Barnes with the mailbag in hand. Mr. Barnes turned, scanned the crowd, and locked eyes with Charlotte, motioning her forward. She felt heat rising to her cheeks as she strode to the front.

"Charlotte, can you jump into the photo, please?"

She sighed. "I knew you were going to ask that."

She stood between Sam and Kendall, posing for a few photos, wrapping her arms around their shoulders as she did. And just when Charlotte was sure her face would crack in half from the smiling, Bob approached.

"Okay, Char, it's about to start. Hannah is saving us seats in the third row."

They found their seats, and Pastor Evans opened the evening with a prayer. Then he picked up the school bell, ringing it once. Its tone was strong and clear, echoing around the room, getting everyone's attention.

The bell was louder than he expected, and Pastor Evans winced. Laughter filled the room and then died down.

"Wow! That works well. I might just use it at the start of Sunday morning services."

More laughter.

"This evening we are going to let you explore our open house. Many of you have told me that you read about it in the article written by Christopher Slater. Christopher, come here."

Christopher's cheeks flushed pink as he walked to the

front of the room. He waved and smiled, and laughter and applause filled the room. Then he bowed and hurried back to his seat.

When the applause died down, Pastor Evans continued. "We decided that since there were so many fascinating items, we wouldn't just put up one display but many. The whole church is open—even my office—although you'll have to overlook the piles of stuff on my desk!

"In each room you'll find a display. In some rooms, like the sanctuary, there will be a series of displays. Most of the items were found in our basement and closets and all the other places we tuck away things when we don't know what to do with them. The ladies of our church found beauty in the hidden things. They put some order to it. And that order brings the history of our church alive. From the 1920s church cookbook in the kitchen to the 1970s flannel graphs in the Sunday school room.

"We also have a special presentation. In a few moments, members of the Stevenson family are going to share the history of a state, a railroad, a depot, a town, a church, and a family. I know you will enjoy it.

"Oh, yes, and I can't sit down without saying one more thing. If you are here tonight and you don't have a church home—a special community with which to worship God—we'd love to have you. We truly are a family that cares for each other—in the challenging times as well as the good.

"Now, please help me welcome Emily, Lily, and Andrea."

Applause sounded from around the room accented by whoops and hollers coming from the back. Charlotte didn't have to turn around to know it was Sam and Pete making all that noise. *Those guys.* She smiled.

The girls approached the front of the room, finding their places. Charlotte held her breath, waiting for Emily to start, hoping she wasn't nervous, and praying she didn't forget what she had to say.

Emily smiled and scanned the crowd, and Charlotte wondered when she'd gotten so grown up.

"Some early pioneers traveled to Nebraska in covered wagons. Even more came on trains. The first railroad was completed across the state in 1867. By 1880 there were 1,868 miles of track."

For the next thirty minutes, Emily, Lily, and Andrea, and later Christopher, Sam, and Kendall, told the story of the "history mystery" that had been in the paper. It started with Christopher talking about the facts from the old newspapers, and then everyone jumped in with the clues that led them to discover the bag under the floorboards.

"This is the metal detector we used," Kendall said with a smile. "I know what you're thinking—maybe we should start going through the basements of more Bedford homes. Believe me, my dad and I have talked about it."

Everyone laughed.

Kendall shuffled her slipper shoes on the faded carpet. "So if there are any takers, please get in touch with us. We love a good treasure hunt."

Laughter again filled the room.

As they finished, applause erupted, and many stood to show their appreciation.

Then the school bell rang again, not once but three

times. Everyone looked around, and Charlotte noticed it was Edna who now carried it. She fluttered to the front of the room holding some type of plaque.

"What you have heard and read from the *Bedford Leader*, of course, is that Elijah Coleman has been officially cleared of all wrongdoing. You may have also heard that the Bedford Community Church has benefited from the sale of historical documents and that all family members we have tracked down have received copies of the letters their ancestors wrote," Edna said. "But what no one knows except me, Pastor Evans, and the library staff is that our new museum room at the library will be called the Elijah Coleman Room."

Applause again filled the room, and this time Charlotte couldn't keep the tears from tumbling down. A dozen sets of arms circled around her, and Charlotte didn't know whose they were. It didn't matter. This was her community, her church. And to her the embrace wasn't just for her; it was for Elijah and Lavina too.

THE PEOPLE MOVED around the fellowship room, in and out to other parts of the church. Except for the weddings of a few of Bedford's prominent citizens, Charlotte had never seen the place so packed. She made her way to the punch bowl, taking one step at a time. "Excuse me. Pardon me."

Mary Louise Henner poured her a cup of punch but didn't really see her as she was busy telling the clerk from the grocery store how she'd been there when they first came across Lavina's journal.

Charlotte smiled to herself and took a step back, trying to figure out where to go next, when Dana approached with her mom, her dad, and Pete.

"The girls did a fantastic job, and the more I get to know this family, the more I just love you all," said Dana's mother. "In fact, I was talking with Pete and the name Elijah has really grown on me. It would be a great name for a son."

Pete nodded, even though Charlotte could tell by the look in his eyes that he wasn't sold on the idea.

"Elijah? That sounds like the name of a sixty-year-old man, not a little boy," Bob cut in.

"Here we go again," Pete mumbled.

"Why, I think Elijah is a fine name for a boy," Charlotte said.

Charlotte noticed Emily and the other girls across the room and realized she hadn't congratulated them yet on a job well done. She turned to Dana and Pete. "Will you excuse me for a minute? I see some girls over there I want to congratulate."

"Sure, Mom."

Charlotte hurried over and noticed they were surrounded by some of their friends, including Ashley, who nearly bounced with excitement.

"It was even better than our presentation—and you didn't even have food!"

Charlotte gave Emily a hug and then patted the shoulders of Andrea and Lily. "Great job. I couldn't be prouder."

"Thanks. I can't wait to return to my school back in the Czech Republic. I am going to see if I can use this material in one of my classes there—two grades for only working once!"

Lily didn't look quite so excited. "Yeah, I suppose we did okay." Charlotte noticed she was eyeing someone across the room. Peeking over her shoulder, Charlotte saw Allison Cunningham and her mother, and instantly Charlotte knew what Lily was waiting for—their approval, their praise. It was clear that even if everyone in this building were to congratulate and tell Lily it was the best thing ever, she wouldn't believe it until she heard it from her mom and grandma.

Charlotte stood there for a moment, wondering if she should butt in and head over there to urge the two women to talk to Lily. Thankfully, she didn't have to, because as Andrea launched into a story about her own school, Allison and Grandma M approached.

Grandma M opened her arms wide. "Girls, that was wonderful. That was—"

"Perfect?" Lily bit her lip.

"Yes, perfect."

Lily's face brightened. "Yes! Success again." She punched the air, but even though she was being playful, Charlotte could see the relief was deeply felt.

"Oh, we weren't wanting to be perfect," Emily quickly added. "We are just glad we were able to tell a story that matters."

"I agree." Andrea nodded. "But we did a super job."

They chatted for a minute about the turnout of the crowd, and Charlotte did her best to mingle. Once the crowd thinned, Charlotte finally had the chance to walk around the church, taking in the displays in each room. She smiled at the large display in the foyer. Someone had taken Maxie's photo of her wedding reception and blown it up to poster size. Even though the faces were grainy and slightly blurry, their smiles were clear, and their eyes were full of joy and hope. On the display board next to the photo, someone had written a caption in beautiful script:

> Perseverance, endurance, and willingness to withstand hardships were among the characteristics possessed by early settlers. Their trials only made them more caring and kinder. Neighborliness became the outstanding virtue.

Charlotte heard footsteps approaching. She turned and noticed Dana hurrying toward her.

"There you are. Are you busy? I hope not because there's something I want to show you. It's in the sanctuary."

As they walked in, Pete was waiting at the top of the aisle and Charlotte got a glimpse of what it would be like just a little over a month from now.

"You haven't seen this yet, have you?" Pete asked, pointing to the display near the altar.

Charlotte sucked in a breath as she saw the wedding dress. It was simple, made of white satin—discolored because of its age—and trimmed with fine lace.

"It belonged to Anita's great-aunt, Peggy. She lent it to the church to use. Isn't it lovely?"

"Yes." Charlotte approached but didn't touch it. She thought of the young woman in her letters and tried to imagine the excitement in her gaze as she put on the dress, knowing Gregory was waiting for her at the end of the aisle.

"But that's not the best part. There's a picture. I hope you don't mind, but I found it in the back of Lavina's Bible that day when Christopher and I were going over all the clues. I told him not to tell you about it, and he promised he wouldn't."

"No, he didn't."

"I'm so glad, because I wanted to do something with Elijah and Lavina's wedding picture."

"Wedding picture?" Charlotte leaned closer. "I have a copy of their engagement picture somewhere, but I don't remember ever seeing her wedding picture."

"That's because it's been in the church basement all this time. Hidden in the Bible, just waiting to be found."

"Among other things," Pete added.

Charlotte looked closer. It showed the young couple side by side. Elijah had dark hair and a boyish face. He wore a dark suit and sat casually with one leg partly crossed over the other and his hands relaxing on his lap. But it was Lavina who caused Charlotte to giggle. She wore a simple Victorian gown with a high collar. Her white-gloved hands were crossed on her lap, but the best part was the look on her face. She was looking down slightly, peering up at the camera under long eyelashes. And her smile! It was soft and playful. With one glance Charlotte knew Lavina was someone she would have loved to meet. The look was sweet, innocent, and excited, and she had a gaze full of adventure.

"This picture . . ." Charlotte was at a loss for words.

"Perfect, isn't it? That is why we decided to put it on our wedding program—in addition to our photo. Here's a proof. What do you think?"

"Together Forever: A Heritage of Love," the program read, with Elijah and Lavina's picture on the front.

Then, when Charlotte opened it she saw a photo of Pete and Dana in their everyday clothes, copying the pose.

"Isn't it great? Emily took the photo with her camera. And the best part—it was Pete's idea." Dana squeezed Charlotte's arm.

"Who knew? Who would have guessed?" Charlotte gazed at her son and noticed his bright eyes and wide smile.

"Who would have guessed is right," Dana said. "Then again, he comes from good roots." She sighed. "A vine of faith and family that will live on for generations."

About the Author

Tricia Goyer is a wife, homeschooling mom, speaker, podcast host, and bestselling author of over 80 books. Tricia writes in numerous genres including fiction, parenting, marriage, and books forchildren and teens. She loves to mentor writers. Married to John and mom of tenchildren, Tricia truly believes teaching and guiding herchildren daily is her greatest work. Tricia lives near Little Rock, Arkansas.

A Note from the Editors

We hope you enjoyed this volume in the Home to Heather Creek series, published by Guideposts. For over seventy-five years, Guideposts, a non-profit organization, has been driven by a vision of a world filled with hope. We aspire to be the voice of a trusted friend, a friend who makes you feel more hopeful and connected.

By making a purchase from Guideposts, you join our community in touching millions of lives, inspiring them to believe that all things are possible through faith, hope, and prayer. Your continued support allows us to provide uplifting resources to those in need.

Whether through our online communities, websites, apps, or publications, we strive to inspire our audiences, bring them together, and comfort, uplift, entertain, and guide them.

To learn more, please go to guideposts.org.

Find inspiration, find faith, find Guideposts.

Shop our best sellers and favorites at
guideposts.org/shop

Or scan the QR code to go directly to our Shop